Peter Rc

Tolkien

Proceedings of The Tolkien Society
Seminar 1996

Edited by Richard Crawshaw
and
Shaun Gunner

Copyright © 2021 by The Tolkien Society
www.tolkiensociety.org

First published 2021 by Luna Press Publishing, Edinburgh
www.lunapresspublishing.com

ISBN-13: 978-1-913387-55-6.

Cover illustration *Earendil* © Alarie
Typesetting @ Francesca Barbini 2021
Published under the auspices of the Peter Roe Memorial Fund, third in the series.

Contents

About the Peter Roe Memorial Fund

The Tolkien Society's seminar proceedings and other booklets are typically published under the auspices of the Peter Roe Memorial Fund, a fund in the Society's accounts that commemorates a young member who died in a traffic accident. Peter Roe, a young and very talented person joined the Society in 1979, shortly after his sixteenth birthday. He had discovered Middle-earth some time earlier, and was so inspired by it that he even developed his own system of runes, similar to the Dwarvish Angerthas, but which utilised logical sound values, matching the logical shapes of the runes. Peter was also an accomplished cartographer, and his bedroom was covered with multi-coloured maps of the journeys of the fellowship, plans of Middle-earth, and other drawings.

Peter was also a creative writer in both poetry and prose—the subject being incorporated into his own *Dwarvish Chronicles*. He was so enthusiastic about having joined the Society that he had written a letter ordering all the available back issues, and was on his way to buy envelopes when he was hit by a speeding lorry outside his home.

Sometime later, Jonathan and Lester Simons (at that time Chairman and Membership Secretary respectively) visited Peter's parents to see his room and to look at the work on which he had spent so much care and attention in such a tragically short life. It was obvious that Peter had produced, and would have continued to produce, material of such a high standard as to make a complete booklet, with poetry, calligraphy, stories and cartography. The then committee set up a special account in honour of Peter, with the consent of his parents, which would be the source of finance for the Society's special publications. Over the years a number of members have made generous donations to the fund.

The first publication to be financed by the Peter Roe Memorial Fund was *Some Light on Middle-earth* by Edward Crawford, published in 1985. Subsequent publications have been composed from papers delivered at Tolkien Society workshops and seminars, talks from guest speakers at the Annual Dinner, and collections of the best articles from past issues of *Amon Hen*, the Society's bulletin.

Dwarvish Fragments, an unfinished tale by Peter, was printed in *Mallorn* 15 (September 1980). A standalone collection of Peter's creative endeavours is currently being prepared for publication.

The Peter Roe Series

I   Edward Crawford, *Some Light on Middle-earth*, Peter Roe Series, I (Pinner: The Tolkien Society, 1985)

II   *Leaves from the Tree: Tolkien's Short Fiction*, ed. by Trevor Reynolds, Peter Roe Series, II (London: The Tolkien Society, 1991)

III   *The First and Second Ages*, ed. by Trevor Reynolds, Peter Roe Series, III (London: The Tolkien Society, 1992; Edinburgh: Luna Press Publishing 2020)

IV   *Travel and Communication in Tolkien's Worlds*, ed. by Richard Crawshaw, Peter Roe Series, IV (Swindon: The Tolkien Society, 1996)

V   *Digging Potatoes, Growing Trees: Volume One*, ed. by Helen Armstrong, Peter Roe Series, V (Swindon: The Tolkien Society, 1997)

VI   *Digging Potatoes, Growing Trees: Volume Two*, ed. by Helen Armstrong, Peter Roe Series, VI (Telford: The Tolkien Society, 1998)

VII   *Tolkien, the Sea and Scandinavia*, ed. by Richard Crawshaw, Peter Roe Series, VII (Telford: The Tolkien Society, 1999)

VIII   *The Ways of Creative Mythologies*, ed. by Maria Kuteeva, 2 vols, Peter Roe Series, VIII (Telford: The Tolkien Society, 2000)

IX   *Tolkien: A Mythology for England?*, ed. by Richard Crawshaw, Peter Roe Series, IX (Telford: The Tolkien Society, 2000)

.

Foreword

When readers think about the places in J.R.R. Tolkien's stories, they mind's eye might be drawn to the journey of Thorin and Company that go over hill and under hill to reach the Lonely Mountain, or that of Frodo and Sam from the Shire to Mordor.

But the sea is also a key literary device in several of Tolkien's narratives: whether that be the journey of the Eldar across the Sea to Aman, and then the Exile of the Noldor back to Beleriand; the journeys of the Númenóreans, most notably those told in "Aldarion and Erendis: The Mariner's Wife"; or the voyages into the West of both Frodo and Eärendil. All of these capture the imagination of readers, who are intrigued by the sense of both danger and adventure that the sea often presents.

But, perhaps none more so that the Downfall of Númenor, the Akallabêth. Not only does the Downfall bring about the tragic end of the great kingdom of Númenor, it also seems to have a parallel in Tolkien's own dreams. In Letter 257 of *The Letters of J.R.R. Tolkien*, he wrote to Christopher Bretherton: "In sleep I had the dreadful dream of the ineluctable Wave, either coming out of the quiet sea, or coming in towering over the green inlands. It still occurs occasionally, though now exorcized by writing about it. It always ends by surrender, and I awake gasping out of deep water." For many, this will bring to mind Tar-Míriel atop Meneltarma as the wave approaches.

The Tolkien Society is a charity based in the UK that has the aim of promoting research into, and educating the public in, the life and works of J.R.R. Tolkien. For over 50 years the Society has worked to publish the latest thinking and research on Tolkien's works, and a cornerstone of this is the *Peter Roe* series of publications which regularly include the proceedings of our Seminars.

Realising the significance in Tolkien's works, the Society held its annual Seminar on the subject "Tolkien, the Sea, and Scandinavia" at the George Hotel in Colchester on 15 June 1996. The Seminars provide an opportunity for scholars and researchers to present their thinking, and engage the community in a discussion on a particular aspect of J.R.R. Tolkien's life and works. The Seminar in 1996 was no exception, and this collection presents five papers delivered at that event.

The first article, "The Wave and Other Dreams in *The Lord of the Rings*" by Patricia Reynolds, looks very directly at the dreams not just in *The Lord of the Rings* but also in "The Notion Club Papers", and argues that Tolkien was doing something more profound than just a nice-sounding trope. "Seas and Shores: A Study of Cataclysms in Middle-earth", by Alex Lewis, poses the question as to how physically and geologically the changes of the world that happen at the ends of the Ages take place. The third article, "Searching for an Earthly Paradise: Some Common Images in the Works of J.R.R. Tolkien and C.S. Lewis" by Maria Kuteeva persuasively argues that the legend of Saint Brendan in search of an Earthly Paradise was discussed between Tolkien and Lewis, and had a particular impact on the latter's works. "The Sea-Bell: A Voyage of Exploration", by Christine Davidson, contrasts the poem from *The Adventures of Tom Bombadil* with Samuel Taylor Coleridge's "The Rime of the Ancient Mariner" amongst others, and how, perhaps, the sea journeys are not just physical, but metaphorical as well. Finally, "Tolkien-on-Sea: The View from the Shores on Middle-earth" by John Ellison brings everything together and looks at Tolkien's creative journey in his writings of the legends and mythology that surround the sea, and the significance this has on understanding Tolkien.

This second edition has been further edited by myself, correcting errors in the original printing as well as amending the name of the book to better reflect the contents. I extend my thanks to Richard Crawshaw, the editor of the first edition, as well as repeat his thanks to Alan Butcher, John Ellison, Maria Kuteeva, Trevor Reynolds, and Andrew Wells.

What has not changed in this second edition is the focus: Tolkien and the Sea. Understanding what Tolkien was trying to achieve with his sea imagery, and what may have led him to include it in his stories continues to be a source of inquiry for Tolkien scholars and readers. This book does help advance our thinking on the life and works of J.R.R. Tolkien, which is why I am pleased to present the republication of this book.

Shaun Gunner
Tolkien Society Chair
February 2021

The Great Wave and Other Dreams in
The Lord of the Rings

Patricia Reynolds[1]

Dreams in *The Lord of the Rings* (Tolkien, 1954/5) are part of a larger theme which permeates that work: the theme of vision or sight. This theme encompasses the far-sight of the Palantír, the long-sight of the Elves, the mystic vision of Galadriel's mirror, the insights of story-telling and poetry. It deals with perception, which is at the heart of fantasy.

The critic Peter Levi (1986, p. 27) has pointed out that visions and not part of mainstream literature:

> Very few visionary poets can be called classical. That is because visions and revelations occur mostly on the outer limits of a given culture, they belong to the deprived and the unrecognised and to those who cultivate secret wisdom… Our own culture rests on reason and on science, our morality is practical and our philosophy is distrustful of visions. If we are still hungry for visions we seek them in the realm of poetry. There, on the outer limits of our culture, we allow them to exist.

1. Thanks are due to the members of Mundeli Sernieva, the Societá Tolkieniana Italiana, and the Tolkien Society, who patiently heard these ramblings (none more than twice!). I owe them much.

Joe R Christopher (1996, p. 122) point out one way in which Tolkien is able to include visions within *The Lord of the Rings*:

> A reader… notices the word *seemed*. "He *seemed* to have grown… it seemed to the eyes of Legolas that a white flame flickered…" This is typical of Tolkien's handling of these moments: in Galadriel's rejection of the Ring, she stands, "*seeming* now tall beyond measurement"; …, if the sleepers had "seen him, they *would have thought* [him] an old weary hobbit…" (emphasis added)
>
> They allow a reader to intellectually deny the vision that, nevertheless, affects his or her emotional response to the book.

Dreams have a similar function: they are one step further from the naturalistic, realistic novel, one step closer to the visionary poem. The reader can still, intellectually, deny the vision. For example, the reader can ascribe the dream to some theory of dreaming, such as the subconscious knowledge of the dreamer, brought to the attention of the conscious in the Jungian manner, or put it down to eating cheese before supper. In presenting his characters' dreams, Tolkien also includes for the reader some hints about theories of dreaming which the reader may use. It is important therefore, to look at the question 'what is a dream', as it is answered in *The Lord of the Rings*.

I think that it is significant that the first dream mentioned in *The Lord of the Rings* occurs very early on, in the second chapter: we have ended 'A Long-Expected Party' with Bilbo's disappearance, and things are beginning to happen.

> He found himself wondering at times, especially in the autumn, about the wild lands, and strange visions of mountains that he had never seen came into his dreams. He began to say to

himself: 'Perhaps I shall cross the river myself one day.' To which the other half of his mind always replied: 'Not yet'.

The structural purpose of these dreams is to prompt the reader to imagine where Bilbo has gone, and perhaps to suggest that Frodo will follow him. The reader may recollect the timing of the dreams when, later in the chapter, Frodo sets out in autumn.

Tolkien tells us little about the mechanics of this dream, but some things can be deduced. Firstly: Frodo sees what he has never seen. Is Frodo's spirit seeking after Bilbo? Many cultures believe that the soul or spirit leaves the body during dreams. Secondly, Frodo's dream is reported almost as a result of his thinking about Bilbo. Most dreamers can point to such external stimuli for at least some parts of some dreams. It is quickly followed by the idea that he has 'two minds'. This is an English idiom 'to be in two minds about something', but it also has the psychological meaning, of conscious and unconscious minds.

It appears that Frodo is not the only one who dreams of mountains: on seeing the Misty Mountains, Gimli says "'Only once before have I seen them from afar in waking life'" (Tolkien, 1954/5, "The Ring Goes South"). The implication is that Gimli has seen them also in dreams, dreams which are a result of his longing, having once seen the mountains.

The second mention of dreams occurs a little further on, in "Three is Company", where "Sam walked along at Frodo's side, as if in a dream" and "Pippin afterwards recalled little … the sound of voices so various and so beautiful that he felt in a waking dreams". This is their reaction to meeting Elves. Although we do not know it for many chapters – not until "The Riders of Rohan" the companions have experienced something

3

close to the dreams of elves, which are unlike the dreams of men.

Dreams and visions are to Elves less mystical than they are for mortals. Elvish dream-sight ranges from the wraith-world to the blessed land. Sight into other-worlds seems more like an extension of their ability to discern the numbers of a company many leagues distant than a mystical experience. Such dreams are as sustaining as sleep, and bear a similar relationship to human dreams that lembas does to cram.

The first visionary dream of Frodo's that we see through his eyes occurs at Crickhollow:

> Eventually he fell into a vague dream, in which he seemed to be looking out of a high window over a dark sea of tangled trees. Down below among the roots there was the sound of creatures crawling and snuffling. He felt sure they would seek him out sooner or later.
>
> Then he heard a noise in the distance. At first he thought it was a great wind coming over the leaves of the forest. Then he knew that it was not leaves, but the sound of the Sea far-off; a sound he had never heard in waking life, though it had often troubled his dreams. Suddenly he found he was out in the open. There were no trees after all. He was on a dark heath, and there was a strange salt smell in the air. Looking up he saw before him a tall white tower, standing alone on a high ridge. A great desire came over him to climb the tower and see the Sea. He started to struggle up the ridge towards the tower: but suddenly a light came in the sky, and there was a noise of thunder.

Well, you hardly need to read the rest of the book, do you? To those re-reading the book, the symbols of towers, trees and sea, the sniffing Black Riders and the noise of thunder are very powerful reminders of what will happen.

To the reader encountering this for the first time, the experience is different. Firstly, there are the snuffling creatures, which the reader can readily identify as Black Riders: and Frodo's knowledge that "they would seek him out sooner or later". They are seeking him in a wood: and Frodo is about to go into a wood, so the reader is being prepared for a fright in the Old Forest. Into this climate of fear, the Sea is introduced into the novel,[2] but we are told that Frodo has dreamt of it before. Writing as the anonymous 'editor' of a selection of poems from the Red Book of Westmarch,[3] Tolkien says "The thought of the Sea was ever-present in the background of hobbit imagination; but fear of it, and distrust of all Elvish lore, was the prevailing mood in the Shire at the end of the Third Age". The theme of sea-longing is taken up again much later, when Legolas sees gulls, and loses his peace of mind.

Light is an important element in dreams and visions throughout the novel. Paul Bibire (1988) has examined the recurrent image of fire through *The Hobbit* and the first four books of *The Lord of the Rings*. Sometimes the fire is hell fire and sometimes the fire of divinity is to be seen in the flames. But above all, light is needed to see. In "The Notion Club Papers", Ramer is reported as saying that light is the method by which the dreamer can move in space and time (Tolkien, 1992, p. 198).

In the encounter with Old Man Willow only Frodo is described as "half in a dream", but all feel sleepy, and all but

2. This is not quite the sea's first implied occurrence: the Grey Havens are mentioned earlier.
3. i.e. The Prologue to *The Adventures of Tom Bombadil*. (Tolkien, 1962).

Sam do fall asleep. This slumber is described by Jane Chance (1992) as "closer to death and unnatural in the middle of the day", and is specifically described by Tolkien as unnatural, through the thoughts of Sam, who comments "'There's more behind this than sun and warm air'".

In the "House of Tom Bombadil" the dreams of all the characters are told (Tolkien, 1954/5). All the dreams are said to be prompted, at least in part, by external noises.

Frodo's is the clearest. He sees Gandalf being taken from Orthanc by Gwaihir (although he does not know that this is what he sees). He then hears riders from the East, and wakes, wondering if he will have the courage to leave Tom Bombadil's house.

Pippin first "lay dreaming pleasantly" and the "woke, or thought he had waked" and hears creaking and tip-tapping, and believes himself back inside Old Man Willow. The soft pillow, and recollection of Tom's words comfort him, and he falls asleep again.

Merry hears water "falling into his quiet sleep" and fears drowning. The hard flagstones and recollection of Tom's words comfort him, and he falls asleep again.

Merry and Pippin have had a version of the same dream: they recollect their encounter with Old Man Willow in a nightmare, but physical reality and Tom's words drive it out. It is possible to see the taps and water as an actual attack by the Old Forest, defeat by the power of Tom Bombadil. These are inconsequential dreams: without portent. It is significant that Sam does not dream: he is not highly-strung and imaginative like Merry and Pippin, his brain does not work away at things as theirs do. He is said to 'sleep like a log': which is ironic, given that Merry and Pippin's dreams are related to Old Man Willow.

6

Frodo's dream, for the first-time reader appears as symbolic as the Crickhollow dream: again we have a tower. Where the first dream was dark, this starts dark, until it is illuminated at moonrise. Things seem to have stepped up a notch: where before snuffling creatures threatened to seek Frodo out, now there are winged creatures, and wolves, and voices, and horses galloping from the East. It is a more violent scene, but a less personal one. The dreamer has left the Shire in his dreams, and is moving out into the wider world.

The second night at Tom Bombadil's house they did not hear noises (Tolkien, 1954/5, "Fog on the Barrow-downs").

> But either in his dreams or out of them, he could not tell which, Frodo heard a sweet singing in his mind: a song that seemed to come like a pale light behind a grey rain-curtain, and growing stronger to turn the veil all to glass and silver, until at last it was rolled back, and a far green country opened under a swift sunrise.
> The vision melted into waking; and there was Tom whistling like a tree-full of birds...

At this point, the reader has no idea what this dream or vision portends. It might not even be a dream. However, in "The Notion Club Papers" dreaming is described in remarkably similar language:

> I felt that it was like the difference between a bright glimpse of a distant landscape: threadlike waters really falling ... between that and any picture" (Tolkien, 1992, p. 172).

But in *The Lord of the Rings* the ambiguity remains. We are told in the next paragraph that the sun had risen, and "Outside everything was green and pale gold". The pale light which turns to swift sunrise can be seen, at least, as a positive sign. The green country could be the fair lands ahead at Rivendell. But there is more than this. Symbolically, the vision of a green countryside, refers to heaven, as in the medieval poem 'Pearl':

> The wondrous wealth of down and dales
> of wood and water and lordly plain…
> (Tolkien, 1975, p. 92, stanza 11)

The rolling-back of the rain-curtain can also be seen on a more psychological level, as the rolling-back of Frodo's fears.

On the Barrow-dawns, as in the Old Forest, the hobbits' sight becomes confused. Merry says his recollections of the attack of the men at Carn Dûm are something he dreamt, and when Tom Bombadil tells them some ancient history

> The hobbits did not understand his words, but as he spoke they had a vision... Then the vision faded, and they were back in the sunlit world (Tolkien, 1954/5, "Fog on the Barrow-downs").

This is the first of many visions and dreams which are contrasted to the 'sunlit world': but note that the vision *faded* – suggesting that the vision itself was no dim apparition, but as bright as sunlight.

When rescued from a Black Rider by Nob in Bree (Tolkien, 1954/5, "Strider"), Merry said "I had an ugly dream, which I can't remember". But Nob has just reported Merry's words on waking, so the reader knows exactly what dream he had: he has had a repeat of his Old Man Willow dream.

Also at the Prancing Pony at Bree, Frodo:

dreams were again troubled with the noise of wind and galloping hoofs. The wind seemed to be curling round the house and shaking it; and far off he heard a horn blowing wildly (Tolkien, 1954/5, "A Knife in the Dark").

This dream ties together the wind from the Crickhollow dream, and the hoofs from the House of Tom Bombadil dream. But it is also a vision of what is happening at Crickhollow: the Black Riders are attacking, and the alarm horn is being blown.

Only one dream of Frodo's is mentioned on the road from Weathertop to Rivendell: he spends a bad night, imagining that the Black Riders are again creeping up on him.

This is before Gandalf explains that wearing the Ring, the real world dims, and the wraith-world becomes clear, (Tolkien, 1954/5, "Many Meetings") where the vision, such as presented by Tom, is a light-full alternative to daylight, the Ring-sight is an alternative to nightmare shadows.

When Frodo wakes in Rivendell, he first thinks that "he had slept late, after a long unpleasant dream that still hovered on the edge of memory" (Tolkien, 1954/5, "Many Meetings"), and the following day reports "yesterday I dreamed that my task was done, and I could rest here, a long while, perhaps for good" (Tolkien, 1954/5, "The Ring Goes South").

Confusion between dreaming and experiencing becomes greater and greater as the novel progresses. As the confusion is resolved at Rivendell, it can be seen that it stems from wearing the ring and the attack by the Nazgûl knife.

Boromir was prompted to go to Rivendell by a dream:

For on the eve of the sudden assault a dream came to my
brother in a troubled sleep; and afterward a like dream came
to him again, and once to me.
In that dream I thought the eastern sky grew dark and there
was a growing thunder, but in the West a pale light lingered,
and out of it I heard a voice, remote but clear, crying:
Seek for the Sword that was broken:

In Imladris it dwells;
There shall be councils taken
Stronger than Morgul-spells
There shall be shown a token
That Doom is near at hand,
For Isildur's Bane shall waken,
And the Halfling forth shall stand.

There are several things to note about this dream. Firstly, it
is not, initially, *Boromir*'s dream, it is *Faramir*'s. I cannot help
but wonder, in the light of following events, if Boromir even
had this dream at all, but merely told Denethor that he did, in
order to be the one sent to Rivendell.

Secondly, the thunder and light tie it to Frodo's dreams,
which prompts the reader to believe that perhaps the same,
good, external force hinted at by Gandalf at the beginning of
the book is at work here, too.

Thirdly, it is, more clearly than anything we have read so
far, a prophetic dream. We are already into the third line of the
verse, the sword has been sought in Imladris, and the council
is, even now, being taken. Everything in this verse appears
clear, but the full force of the Morgul-spells has yet to be
seen.

When Gandalf reports his experience on Orthanc to the

council, Frodo immediately recognises it, probably from his dream in the House of Tom Bombadil. I say probably, because in the report of that dream, we are told that Frodo saw Gandalf's release, and what he recalls now occurred before his release:

> 'I saw you!' cried Frodo. 'You were walking backwards and forwards. The moon shone in your hair.'
> Gandalf paused astonished and looked at him. 'It was only a dream,' said Frodo... (Tolkien, 1954/5, "The Council of Elrond")

Now, what is Gandalf's reaction to this: further amazement, or asking what else Frodo has dreamed, and may be of interest to the council? Or perhaps a dismissal of the dream as a coincidence. No – just a mild ticking-off for whoever is in control of dreams: "'it was late in coming'", for this dream should have prompted Frodo to leave the Shire. It is not at all clear whether Frodo himself should have given himself this dream, or whether someone else should have sent it. Following on, as it does, from Faramir's dream, there is a strong suggestion that 'someone else' was responsible.

It is, I think, significant, that the very next dream Frodo has comes bang on time. On the shoulder of Caradhras the Cruel, Frodo

> felt himself sinking fast into a warm and hazy dream. He thought a fire was heating his toes, and out of the shadows on the other side of the hearts he heard Bilbo's voice speaking. *I don't think much of your diary*, he said. *Snowstorms on January the twelfth: there was no need to come back to report that!*
> *But I wanted rest and sleep, Bilbo*, Frodo answered with an effort.

This is the very argument which Frodo has to present to his companions as soon as they have retreated from the mountain: how can they return without shame, unless they have been defeated (Tolkien, 1954/5, "A Journey in the Dark"). Also note the psychological reality in this dream: people slipping into hypothermia do believe themselves warm and comfortable, and have been known to actually remove clothing, feeling that it has got too warm.[4]

When Frodo first sees Gollum's luminous eyes in Moria, he believes that he "was on the edge of a dream" (Tolkien, 1954/5, "A Journey in the Dark"), and as they journey down the Great River Sam reports "'I had a funny dream... It was queer. All wrong, if it wasn't a dream'" (Tolkien, 1954/5, "The Great River") when he sees Gollum. Sam is, by this point, not the Hobbit who left the Shire: he has looked into the Mirrormere, Kheled-zâram (Tolkien, 1954/5, "Lothlórien") and been so moved that when Pippin, not believing his own eyes asks the prosaic, straightforward Sam what he has seen, he is unable to answer. Looking into Galadriel's mirror is another stage of his movement towards clear perceptions. But at this point, to Sam, dreams aren't the only place where things can be "All wrong."

Most of the dreams occur in *The Fellowship of the Ring*, more than in *The Two Towers*, and *The Return of the King* together. One of the reasons there are fewer dreams in the second and third volumes is that the company passes into increasingly nightmarish, or dream country. Sam says this clearly in Cirith Ungol:

---

4. I haven't been able to trace when this phenomenon was first reported in the psychological and popular press but I wonder if Tolkien had observed it in the Trenches.

'Am I still dreaming?' he [Frodo] muttered. 'But the other dreams were horrible.'

'You're not dreaming at all, Master,' said Sam. 'It's real. It's me. I've come.'

And after their rescue, in his second true dream, Sam believes himself still asleep in Ithilien.

Full memory flooded back, and Sam cried aloud: 'It wasn't a dream! ...'

The ring-bearers have an elvish quality about them: they experience the real world of bright sunlight, and the veiled world of dream, both waking and sleeping.

Aragorn pays attention to his dreams: he is restless at Parth Galen, and wakes and asks Frodo to draw Sting (Tolkien, 1954/5, "The Breaking of the Fellowship"). Later, as he, Gimli and Legolas pursue the orcs, he hears the hoofbeats of the Riders of Rohan

It comes to my mind that I heard them, even as I lay on the ground in sleep, and they troubled my dreams: horses galloping, passing in the West. But now they are drawing ever further from us, riding northward (Tolkien, 1954/5, "The Riders of Rohan")

This sound is threatening, because of Frodo's dreams of the Black Riders, but they turn out to be the Riders of Rohan.

In *The Two Towers*, Pippin to a certain extent takes over the role of visionary from Frodo.

Captured by orcs, Pippin dreams that he is underground, calling for Frodo, while orc faces surround him. Where Merry

13

simply re-dreamed his Old Man Willow dream, Pippin only carries on the feeling of imprisonment. The tunnels with orcs could be drawn from memories of Moria. And, of course, Pippin finds himself in a very nasty situation. This dream is chilling because it brings Frodo into the situation of orcs' capture which is every bit as terrifying as the dream (Tolkien, 1954/5, "The Uruk-Hai"). Into his ordeal, comes the vision of Aragorn, running behind, which prompts Pippin to run aside for a short way and drop his elf-leaf cloak-pin. As, pages before, we have seen Aragorn running and finding that very same brooch, the vision is as clear to us as it is to Pippin.

Pippin's dream and vision are in part preparing us for his looking into the Palantír (Tolkien, 1954/5, "The Palantír"). There he sees stars, moonlight, and then deep fire (images we should recognise from Frodo's dreams), before contact is made with Sauron.

Pippin's final perception he has, is that he and Gandalf are in fact stationary, and the world is turning beneath their feet and a rushing of wind (Tolkien, 1954/5, "The Palantír"). Again, the wind harks back to Frodo's dream in Crickhollow. When Pippin wakes in Anórien, he cannot tell whether the ride has been entirely a dream or reality – the same confusion between dreaming and existence experienced by Frodo.

Dreaming is not any indicator of moral worth – Orcs dream too: "'You speak of what is deep beyond the reach of your muddy dreams'" says Grishnákh to Uglúk, when he has spoken of the Nazgûl (Tolkien, 1954/5, "The Uruk-Hai").

A pleasant dream comes to Frodo in the Dead Marshes, which refreshes him as Elvish dreams do, (Tolkien, 1954/5, "The Passage of the Marshes") and has an invigorating dream on the road to the Cross-Roads above Osgiliath (Tolkien,

1954/5, "Of Herbs and Stewed Rabbit"). The first is in contrast to the nightmare vision of the dead in the pools, the second almost seems to result from Frodo smelling the rabbits Sam is cooking. At least, it strengthens the positive and optimistic tone of the book at this point.

The title of the following chapter, 'The Window on the West' calls attention to the ties it has with Frodo's nightmare in Bombadil's house, and its opposite, Frodo's vision from the flet in Lothlórien. The waterfall-curtain also recalls the veil of rain from Frodo's later vision in Bombadil's house. But the dreamer in this chapter is not Frodo, but Faramir, who has seen Boromir pass in his death-boat: "'Dreamlike it was, yet no dream, for there was no waking'" (Tolkien, 1954/5, "The Window on the West"). But while Faramir looks for portent and symbol in this dream, the reader knows he sees actuality.

Sam's first true dream is remarkably like his vision in Galadriel's mirror, and also echoes Frodo's dream on the road from Weathertop. He dreams he is searching in the garden at bag End, a garden grown rank. Remembering that he is looking for his pipe, he wakes. Against the cumulative images of the Shire under threat and his great weariness, the pipe is almost a comic touch; there is something of Bilbo's hankering after the comforts of home in *The Hobbit* about it. But we are quickly reminded that Sam might have a pipe in his pack, but he has no leaf, and he is miles from home. The effect of this is to make Sam's dream even more a dream of despair.

A minor dreaming sequence, occurs in the Houses of Healing at Minas Tirith:

Still at whiles as the morning wore away they would speak, murmuring in their dreams; and the watchers listened to all that they said, hoping perhaps to learn something that would help them to understand their hurts (Tolkien, 1954/5, "The Houses of Healing")

And it appears that this, had it been possible before the shadows lengthened, might have been some help, because Éowyn was despairing because she thought Éomer dead (Tolkien, 1954/5, "The Houses of Healing"). There is reference to the theory that the dream related to physical health: that the doctor could diagnose the illness, its causes, or its treatment from a dream, which was first advanced by Aristotle.

On the last approach to Mount Doom, dreams occur again. Frodo dreams of fire (Tolkien, 1954/5, "The Land of Shadow"), Sam dreams of 'dark creeping shapes', and sees 'lights like gloating eyes' (Tolkien, 1954/5, "Mount Doom") – eyes which are also seen when he is awake – by now well known to the reader as being Gollum.

Sam has now passed from prosaic Hobbit, through dreamer, to Visionary.

After the destruction of the Ring, Sam sees a full vision (Tolkien, 1954/5, "Mount Doom"):

Towers fell and mountains slid; walls crumbled and melted, crashing down; vast spires of smoke and spouting steam went billowing up, up, until they toppled like an overwhelming wave and its wild crest curled and came foaming down on the land. And then at last over the miles between there came a rumble, rising to a deafening crash and roar; the earth shook, the plain heaved and cracked, and Orodruin reeled. Fire belched from its riven summit. The skies burst into thunder seared with lightening. Down like lashing whips fell a torrent of black rain.

Sam now confuses dream and existence, in the passage mentioned above where he dreams of Gollum's eyes.

This vision draws on the earlier dreams. The fire image is here taken to its ultimate end: destroying everything. The fire here is fire of hell. But, a little of the sea imagery is retained in the giant wave. On first reading this, the source of the image, in the drowning of Númenor, is not seen: rather, it harks back to the threatening, unearthly quality of the sea in Frodo's early dreams.

Only two chapters later (Tolkien, 1954/5, "The Steward and the King"), Faramir tells Éowyn of the Great Wave coming upon Númenor as they stood on the walls of Minas Tirith when the Ring was destroyed. Faramir 'wondered to hear himself speak' of such things, although he has 'often' dreamed them, and further says: 'It was but a picture in the mind. I do not know what is happening'.

In a letter written in response to a request by W.H. Auden for material which Tolkien would like to see included in a talk about *The Lord of the Rings*, Tolkien wrote that he had an 'Atlantis complex': he dreamed of 'the Great Wave, towering up, and coming in ineluctably over the trees and green fields'.

Tolkien continued in that letter:

(I bequeathed it to Faramir.) I don't think I have had it since I wrote the 'Downfall of Númenor' as the last of the legends of the First and Second Age. (1981, p. 213)

It is actually rather difficult to identify which of his writings Tolkien is referring to, here. There is no writing with exactly this title. One might expect it to be 'The Fall of Númenor', but the first version (Tolkien, 1987, pp. 15-16) mentions no wave.

This texts dates to before the autumn of 1937. At some point before this date Tolkien had a conversation with Lewis about time and space travel, which lead to *The Lost Road* and *Out of the Silent Planet*.[5] In this original outline (Tolkien, 1987, p. 11) Númenor is called Atlantë. In the earliest full version, FN1, 'Númenor was utterly thrown down and overwhelmed in sea' (p. 16).

While the full text of the second version is not quoted by Christopher Tolkien, he says that he has noted "the few differences from FN1 that are of any substance" (Tolkien, 1987, p. 27). One striking change is to portion §5, where Sauron arrives on a wave.

At the same time that Tolkien was working on 'The Notion Club Papers'[6] he turned again to Númenor and wrote 'The Drowning of Anadûnê'. The first draft of the "Drowning", like the third version of the "Fall of Númenor" which preceded it, contains no mention of the great wave (Tolkien, 1992, p. 351). That does not happen until the second text, where:

And last of all the mounting wave, green and cold and plumed with foam, took to its bosom Ar-Zimrahil the Queen... (Tolkien, 1992, p. 373)

Christopher finds it 'hard to believe that no drafting intervened between the two' (Tolkien, 1992, p. 357). The

5. The conversation and its dating are discussed in *The Lost Road* (Tolkien, 1987, pp. 7-8).
6. . 'The Notion Club Papers' was written around Christmas 1946, and he may have begun to think about it around Christmas two years previously (Tolkien, 1992, p. 145). That is, it dates from sometime after the starting of Book V of *The Lord of the Rings* in October 1944, but before, in 1947, he was drafting the opening chapters of Book VI.

letter to Auden, where Tolkien specifically mentions the wave was written 7 June 1955, and therefore *could* be referring to something written only a few months before, but the passage does not give the feeling that this was a recent occurrence.

The Númenórean section of *The Lost Road* was transformed over the following years into the 'Akallabêth' of *The Silmarillion*. The first draft of this had its title amended from "The Fall of Númenor" to "The Downfall of Númenor", suggesting that it may have been written before 7 June 1955. Christopher Tolkien does not suggest a date for this manuscript, only saying that the B version was written "after some considerable interval" (Tolkien, 1986, p. 141), and that the C version may have been made in 1958 (Tolkien, 1986, p. 142). In all versions it is described as coming: 'last of all, the mounting wave, green and cold and plumed with foam, climbing over the land, took to its bosom Tar-Míriel the Queen ... the devouring wave rolled over the land and Númenor toppled to its fall...' (Tolkien, 1977, pp. 279-280, and 1996, discussion of paragraph 78, p. 157).

Thus, as far as can be seen (although there is a very strong case for a missing draft or drafts) the first mention of the Great Wave comes not in the mainstream mythology, but in Sam's vision at the Crack of Doom.

For Frodo, dreaming becomes a curse, as he cannot forget the Ring. As Paul Kocher puts it "Waking or asleep, Frodo is afflicted by a second life of memory, much as elves are." (1972, p. 109)

The novel ends with the conclusion of his dream in Tom Bombadil's house: in the same words, and refers back to that dream.

And then it seemed to him that as in his dream in the house of
Bombadil, the grey rain-curtain turned all to silver glass and
was rolled back, and he beheld white shores and beyond them
a far green country under a swift sunrise.

The dream is now both made concrete (as it was in the house
of Tom Bombadil), and the symbolism becomes more apparent.
Drawing back the veil is a metaphor for seeing more clearly,
and is a symbol between the human and divine, founded in the
veil which divides the Holy of Holies from the more secular
parts of the Temple in Jerusalem.[7]
There has been one addition to the Bombadil dream: the
white shores. In placing his paradise over the sea, Tolkien
draws further on the medieval vision of 'Pearl':

For fair as was this hither shore
Far lovelier was the further land.
(Tolkien, 1975, p. 93, stanza 13)

In both *The Lord of the Rings* and *Pearl*, heaven is seen as
more than a garden, it is envisioned as an entire land: it was a
theme Tolkien was working on at this time in *Leaf by Niggle*.[8]
The visionary poetry discussed by Levi has a long tradition.
In the earliest classical and biblical literature[9], the poets echo

7. Tolkien uses the biblical 'raiment' (clothing) to show the way the divine is
presented to physical eyes (Tolkien, 1977, p. 21).
8. Tolkien began work on an edition of 'Pearl' in 1925 (Gordon, 1953, p.
iii), and Christopher Tolkien says that 'A form of the Pearl translation was in
existence more than thirty years ago' [i.e. before 1945] (Tolkien, 1975, p. 7).
9. The word 'dream' is not recorded in Anglo-Saxon. Divination was by
runes rather than by dreams. The only occurrence of a dream in Anglo-Saxon
literature I can find occurs in the poem 'The Wonderer': Often, when grief

the belief of those times – that dreams are communications from the gods. They are very close to visions and to shamanist trances. Sometimes the gods speak clearly, and sometimes through a special, symbolic language. In Homer's *Iliad*, for example, Agamemnon received instructions from Zeus, in a dream. Biblical dreams include Joseph's, Solomon's, and Daniel's. Although in Ecclesiasticus[10] the point is put that

> dreams put fools in a flutter, as well clutch at shadows and chase the wind as put any faith in dreams. Mirror and dream are similar things: confronting a face, the reflection of that face.

The synonyms for dream in the concordance to the *Jerusalem Bible* are telling: Consultation, Divination, manifestation, Revelation.

I think that Tolkien comes close to saying that several dreams – especially Frodo's dream in Tom Bombadil's house, and Faramir's summons to the Council of Elrond are sent by the Valar.

Deirdre Green (1996, p. 46) sees one feature of the dreams in *The Lord of the Rings* as having a biblical source – the dreams:

> are remarkably pictorial. This quality suggests the influence of the apocalyptic books of *The Bible*, in which messages are conveyed not through direct statement but through clusters of complex visual symbols.

---

and sleep combined together enchain the wretched solitary man, it seems to him in his imagination that he is embracing and kissing his lord ... (trans. Bradley, 1982, p. 323).
10. Ecclesiasticus 34, trans: *Jerusalem Bible*.

But this feature may simply reflect the nature of Tolkien's own dreams. Donne, for example, writes of "Subject A ... This subject is an artist, and his resemblances are all of the purely visual kind" (1934, p. 235), and Tolkien's own artistic works are well documented.

Tolkien draws remarkably little on the works of the two great figures of psychology, Jung and Freud, who gave very different emphasis to dreams in the 20th century.

Tolkien effectively dismisses the psychological approach in 'The Notion Club Papers' where Rufus Dolbear is both a close companion to Ramer, and an amateur psychologist, who will 'analyse a whole book as cheerfully as a page' but does not (Tolkien, 1992, p. 183). In the original scheme of the novel, where the members of the Notion Club were closely modelled on members of the Inklings, Dolbear took the place of R.E. Havard, a doctor in general practice.

The Freudian interpretation of dreams is that they are not communicative, that they use symbols which are personal or culturally determined often rooted in infancy. Freud thought dreams were wish-fulfilment, often of an otherwise hidden sexual nature. This isn't how Tolkien sees the world.

Jung seems closer to Tolkien: he sees dreams as messages from the self to the self. Dreams are involved with wish-fulfilment, but are there to enable the dreamer to fulfil his or her wishes.

Tolkien does, to some extent, use Jung: he does use some common symbols, for example the wind, which symbolises speed and danger is common to Frodo's and Pippin's dreams. Tolkien pushes the revelatory function of dreams further, into the visions which Joe Christopher pointed out in a passage quoted earlier are marked by 'seemed'. In his description of

22

his 'Atlantis-haunting' dream as 'beginning with memory', Tolkien seems to me to be referring to the collective memory, in the Jungian sense, because it follows only lines later from the observation 'his heart may remember, even if he has been cut off from all oral tradition, the rumour all along the coasts of the Men out of the Sea.' (Tolkien, 1981, pp. 212-3).[11]

And there is, I suggested earlier, a Jungian interpretation possible for some of Frodo's dreams. But nevertheless, it remains true that the dreams fit better into the Classical or Biblical understanding of dreams. But to explain why, it is necessary first to look at the literature in the middle.

In literature of the Middle Ages, the dream is often used as a framing device. The dream is a window, which the dreamer (and hence the writer and the reader) can use to examine another world. This was popularised in the *Roman de la Rose*. For the author the nature of dreams – the surreal disjunctions, the symbolic language, the traditional association of the visionary with sanctity – make a dream a very useful way to talk about other worlds. (And talking about other worlds is in turn, a way to talk about this world.) In a dream there is no need to follow a storyline, instead the dreamer's sight can be focused on a succession of scenes with no temporal or locational connection: the dreamer and the reader must make the links, if any, between the scenes. The symbolic language of dreams can be utilised to make literal and vivid the symbols which are part of common understanding. The belief that the dreamer is sanctified, that the dream cannot be anything but true, even if that truth is not literal but symbolic, means that the reader is predisposed to

11. Christopher Tolkien, however, says 'By "beginning with memory" I believe that my father meant that the recurrence of the dream went as far back in his life as his memory reached' (Tolkien, 1992, p. 217).

believe what the author says a character dreams is true.

Tolkien is particularly associated with the Medieval Dream poem previously quoted: 'Pearl'. The dreamer is a father whose little daughter has just died. He sleeps on his daughter's grave, and in his dreams, he sees his 'pearl' in heaven.

But Tolkien rejects the dream as a frame in *On Fairy-Stories*:

> I would also exclude [from the fairy-story genre], or rule out of order, any story that uses the machinery of Dream, the dreaming of actual human sleep, to explain the actual occurrence of its marvels. At the least even if the reported dream was in other respects in itself a fairy-story, I would condemn the whole as gravely defective: like a good picture in a disfiguring frame. It is true that Dream is not unconnected with Faerie. In dreams strange powers of the mind may be unlocked. In some of them a man may for a space wield the power of Faery, that power which, even as it conceives the story, causes it to take living form and colour before the eyes. (1964, pp. 17-8)

For the most significant use of dreams as inspirations, we must look back to the classical, to the "artistic posture", as Deirdre Green (1996, p. 46) puts it: the dream-inspired author, which, she observes,

> is, of course, neither singular now new. Whereas for Aristotle the poet was chiefly a "maker" or craftsman, for Plato "all good poets epic as well as lyric compose their beautiful poems not by art, but because they are inspired and possessed"

Other authors and playwrights who were inspired by their

dreams include makers as diverse as Robert Louis Stevenson,[12] Graham Greene,[13] W.B. Yeats and Jean Cocteau.[14]

In *On Fairy-Stories* (written in 1938-9), Tolkien appears to deny the creativity of dreams:

> Many people ... dislike any meddling with the Primary world ... they, therefore, stupidly, and even maliciously confound Fantasy with Dreaming in which there is no Art.

But in a note, he expounds: 'This is not true of all dreams. In some Fantasy seem to take a part' (1964, p. 45). Tolkien went on to further explore the relation of dreams to literary creation through the character of Ramer in 'The Notion Club Papers', who explains the sources he used in trying to write a space-travel story:

> 'Another thread was dreams. And that had a literary origin, too, partly. Because Rufus and I have long been interested in dreams, especially in their story-and-scene making, and in their relation to waking fiction. But as far as I could judge such things, it did seem to me that a pretty good case had been made out for the view that in a dream a mind can, and sometimes does, move in Time: I mean, can observe a time other than that occupied by the sleeping body during the dream.' (Tolkien, 1992, p. 175)

---

12. 'How often have these sleeping Brownies ['the little people who manage man's internal theatre'] done him honest service, and given him, as he sat idly taking his pleasure in the boxes, better tales than he could fashion for himself' (Stevenson, 1892, quoted in Inglis, 1987, pp. 8-9).

13. 'The unconscious collaborates in all our work: it is a *negre* we keep in the cellar to aid us. When an obstacle seems insurmountable, I read the day's work before sleep and leave the *negre* to labour in my place.' (Graham, 1981, quoted in Inglis, 1987, p.11).

14. See Inglis, 1987, pp. 7-17 for full details.

Alberto Monteiro wrote that Ramer 'is an experimenter in "dreams" which resemble "Astral Projection" (since he can visit other planets!)' and goes on to survey the relationships between Ramer and Tolkien.[15] Astral in this sense means not so much 'having to do with the stars' as 'having to do with the spirit'.[16] In a work which may well have influenced Tolkien,[17] *An Experiment with Time*, J.W. Dunne details how to use dreams to effect time travel. He specifically says that his dreams are not "insanity, clairvoyance, astral-wandering, spirit messages, and telepathy" (1936, p. 48), and goes on to show that by "steadying of attention" it is possible to "slip over the dividing line" while waking (p. 102).

Tolkien put the following words into the mouth of Ramer in 'The Notion Club Papers' (1992, p. 183):

> And I have had also the not uncommon experience of remembering fragments of dreams that seemed to possess a "significance" or emotion that the waking mind could not discern in the remembered scene.

---

15. Alberto Monteiro writes: "He is also a writer, and his biography is so close to T's that it's impossible to think that Ramer's dreams aren't Tolkien's. Example: Ramer was born in Hungary, but his parents returned to England when he was four (like Tolkien, replace Hungary by South Africa). Ramer was a member of an Inkling-like group. And Ramer was a writer. Most likely, some of Ramer's dreams (that he acquired in an unusual, semi-psychotic way) are Tolkien's (but now in more mundane ways). Like Ramer, Tolkien used his dreams as source of inspiration to write his books (the Great wave, for example)."

16. The *Oxford English Dictionary* unfortunately does not record the usage of 'astral projection', nor of 'astral-wandering' (used by Dunne, 1934, p. 48).

17. Or John Buchan's *The Gap in the Curtain* (1932) may be the route of influence – Dunne (1936, p. 241) reports that Buchan says his book was inspired by *An Experiment with Time*.

Christopher writes in a note (p. 215) to this:

Of this experience also my father spoke to me, suggesting, as does Ramer here, that the significance did not lie in the remembered passage itself. (See Ramer's subsequent remarks on this topic, pp. 189ff)

In those pages Ramer strongly relates remembered passage of fiction to passages of dreams. This is particularly significant as Ramer goes on to report:

Here are some of my fragments of this kind. There is the empty throne on the top of a mountain. There is a Green Wave, white-crested, fluted and scallop-shaped but vast, towering above green fields, often with a wood of trees, too; that has constantly appeared [CT's note no. 45]. I saw several times a scene in which a wide plain lay before the feet of a steep ridge on which I stood; the opposing sky was immense, rising as a vertical wall, not bending to a vault, ablaze with stars strewn almost regularly over all its expanse. That is an omen or presage of catastrophe. (Tolkien, 1992, p. 194)

This is Frodo's Crickhollow dream. When asked to explain, Ramer protests that it would take too long to cover 'even one of the immense and ramified legends and cosmogonies that these belong to.' Lowdham asks if not even the Green Wave can be covered. After some further discussion on the nature of dreams and the language "Old Solar", Ramer returns to this subject:

I could tell you a great deal about Atlantis, for instance; though that is not its name to me...
It's connected with that Fluted Wave,' he said; 'and with

another symbol: the Great Door, shaped like a Greek Π with sloping sides.

In the original draft of this passage, Ramer had said 'I could tell you about Atlantis (though that's not its name to me, nor Númenor)' (1992, p. 221), but Tolkien had crossed out 'nor Númenor' "strongly". And the introduction to the name now occurs in Part Two, where Lowdham is – if the word is not too strong – inspired by a cloud, and Ramer reveals it as 'his'[18] name for Atlantis. (Tolkien, 1992, p. 206)

Lowdham is prompted in Part Two to a full vision of the fall of Númenor, which ends:

'Still the eagles pursue us ... The wind is like the end of the world, and the waves are moving. We go into darkness.' (Tolkien, 1992, p. 231)

Lowdham's vision and his reaction to it are remarkably similar to Faramir's.

Yet a further inter-weaving of Middle-earth and the fictionalised Oxford of 'The Notion Club Papers' occurs with the 'Great Storm' of 1987,[19] which seems to have been haunted by Númenor:

'We both heard many tales of the huge waves "high as hills"

---

18. In Part One Ramer and the others have discussed at some length the subject of personal and invented languages.

19. As we know, there was indeed a great storm in 1987, begging the question which is not addressed in the rest of this paper (because asking such questions is beyond the scope of literary criticism): can dreams truly be prophetic? I feel this is one dream, if it is not a literary invention, which Dunne would have rated a 'good' in the 'value' column.

coming in on the Black Night. And curiously enough, many of the tale-tellers agreed that the greatest waves were like phantoms, or only half real: "like shadows of mountains of dark black wicked water" ... one old man ... said that he had seen a tall black ship high on the crest of the great wave, with its masts down and the rags of black and yellow sails flapping on the deck, and great tall me standing on the high poop and wailing...' (Tolkien, 1992, p. 267)

Tolkien saw his writing as sub-creation under God, inspired. And I think Tolkien saw his dreams, especially the Atlantis-haunting, as one, sparking, part of that inspiration, and believing them so, wove them into his fiction.

Bibliography

Bibire, Paul, 1988 'Servant of the Secret Fire' in *Proceedings of the Cambridge Tolkien Workshop 1988*, ed. I.R. Morus, M.J.L. Percival and C.S. Rosenthal.

Bradley, S.A.J., 1982, *Anglo-Saxon Poetry*, London: Dent.

Chance, Jane, 1992, *The Lord of the Rings: The Mythology of Power,* New York: Twayne Publishers.

Christopher, Joe R., 1996 'The Moral Epiphanies in *The Lord of the Rings*' in ed. Patricia Reynolds and Glen Goodknight *Proceedings of the J.R.R. Tolkien Centenary Conference*, Altadena and Milton Keynes: The Mythopoeic Society and the Tolkien Society.

Dunne, J.W., 1936, *An Experiment with Time*, 3rd edition, London: Faber & Faber Ltd.

Gordon, E.V., ed., 1953, *Pearl*, London: Oxford University Press.

Greene, Deirdre, 1996, 'Higher Argument: Tolkien and the tradition of Vision, Epic and Prophecy' in ed. Patricia Reynolds and Glen Goodknight *Proceedings of the J.R.R. Tolkien Centenary Conference*, Altadena and Milton Keynes: The Mythopoeic Society and the Tolkien Society.

Inglis, Brian, 1987, *The Power of Dreams*, London: Grafton Books.

Kocher, Paul, 1972, *Master of Middle-earth: The Achievement of J.R.R. Tolkien*, London: Thames and Hudson.

Levi, Peter, 1986. "Visionary Poets" in *Agenda* XXIV, 3 (Autumn 1986).

Monteiro, Alberto (Dain Ironfoot) albmont@centrooin.com.br ;
tolkien@listproc.hcf.jhu.edu

Stevenson, Robert Louis, 1892, *Across the Plains*.

Tolkien, J.R.R., 1954/5, *The Lord of the Rings*, London: George Allen
& Unwin.
---, 1962, *The Adventures of Tom Bombadil*, London: George Allen
& Unwin.
---, 1964, 'On Fairy-Stories', in *Tree and Leaf*, London: George Allen
& Unwin.
---, 1975, 'Pearl' in *Sir Gawain and the Green Knight, Pearl, and Sir
Orfeo*, London: Unwin Paperbacks.
---, 1977, *The Silmarillion*, London: George Allen & Unwin.
---, 1987, *The Lost Road and Other Writings*, London: Unwin Hyman.
---, 1992, *Sauron Defeated*, London: HarperCollins Publishers.
---, 1996, *The Peoples of Middle-earth*, London: HarperCollins
Publishers.

Seas and Shores: A Study of Cataclysm in Middle-earth

Alex Lewis

It is remarkable to think how much the topography of Middle-earth along the western shores changed in the course of seven thousand years. During the first three Ages of the Sun there were major alterations to mountain ranges, the course of rivers, bays and landing sites, and the shoreline and the limits of the Great Lands themselves.

By comparison, it seems to me that the shores of Valinor changed little, if at all. I would like to investigate some of the physical processes underlying the fictional historical events in order to try and determine the differences between the Great Lands and Valinor.

These changes in the topography brought about profound changes in the way of life of Elves and Men in Middle-earth and beyond. The three Ages were each accompanied by some cataclysmic event: at the end of the First Age there was the Drowning of Beleriand, and at the end of the Second the Drowning of Númenor, and at the end of the Third, the destruction of Mordor. The key event in each case was a volcanic explosion.

*

In the First Age, there was the Ban of the Valar. People could sail south and north and east, but not west to Valinor. Yet the Undying Lands were within physical reach: they had not been sundered as yet. Beleriand was a region beyond the unbroken range of the Blue Mountains (see *The Silmarillion* map) and had many features of note – the Ered Wethrin, a mountain range that ended at a great promontory known as Mount Taras overlooking the sea, great rivers such as the Sirion and Gelion, forest and hills, and of course natural harbours such as the Bay of Balar at the mouths of Sirion. All these lands somehow were inundated at the end of the First Age, the mountain range of the Blue Mountains were torn about and the River Lune driven to pour through this new gap into a new gulf that spilled into the sea. What cataclysm could cause a mountain range to suddenly come apart? There are perhaps two explanations: natural and unnatural causes.

Natural causes would be earthquakes or severe volcanic activity.

Unnatural would be down to something the Dwarves of Nogrod or Belegost (or both) had got up to underground which resulted in the total disruption of the mountain range. The most devastating hydrogen bomb modern man might in his madness wield would probably not bring such a thing about, and I am inclined to suspect natural causes. Severe volcanic activity such as Mount St. Helens in Washington State, USA, and Krakatoa give us potent examples of the force of nature that can blow away a mountain mass in moments.

The entire landmass west of the Blue Mountains collapsed and submerged into the sea – presumably to a depth of at least a hundred feet, else the hills, highlands and other features would have poked up out of the water forming a series of islands.

That there are some parts of the land still there is evident from the map provided in *Unfinished Tales*, where two islands are shown off the coast – Himling, which is what used to be Himring Hill, and Tol Fuin, the highlands of Taur-nu-Fuin. But since neither of these features were the highest in Beleriand, if the process were one of simple submersion due, for instance, to rising sea water levels from global warming, then why do we not see the Ered Wethrin and Mount Taras as islands, or the ring of mountains that encircled Gondolin? The fact that they are not to be found on the map of *Unfinished Tales* lends more credence to a process of plate movement with attendant earthquake activity and perhaps differential subsidence, or of some violent volcanic activity. Also, such a rise in sea levels would take place over far longer periods than the months it seems to have taken: this was not a sudden process in Beleriand as was the case for Númenor, for peoples managed to walk to safety and armies gathered themselves and retreated from Beleriand in good order. Yet it was not a process measured in geological eons either.

Neither volcanic eruption nor earthquakes by themselves, to my mind, can fully account for all the inundation and change of topography to the mountain range, so I am going to suggest that both volcanic activity *and* plate movement came about virtually simultaneously – in geological terms – and one was probably the trigger for the other, and for which for the sake of brevity I shall call the "double-whammy" theory.

If, for instance, the top or side of Mount Dolmed were blown off in a Mount St. Helens-style explosion, and that violent eruption in its wake set off tremors, that might account for all the devastation we see in terms of changes to the landscape. After the eruption of Mount Dolmed, the pressures building up gradually along the tectonic plates surrounding Beleriand might then have been suddenly and catastrophically released, leading to the effects as we know them from examining the map of *The Silmarillion* and comparing it to that of *The Lord of the Rings* – the Ered Luin were pulled apart suddenly and quickly by the explosion, and the whole of Beleriand then drowned to a depth of at least 100 feet. Another reason for the depth suggested is that if there were not areas of Beleriand at that depth, or deeper, the great ships of the Númenóreans in the later age could not have sailed into the Gulf of Lune to meet with Círdan and Gil-galad. Also major fault lines must have existed almost entirely surrounding the mass of Beleriand to account for the whole area subsiding in this way, and one can consider the whole of Beleriand as a single plate of rub-plate.

The main problem existing for the double-whammy scenario is that we have no other indication that the Ered Luin were formed by volcanic processes or that there are active volcanoes in the Blue Mountain range. Indeed, as far as we know, for the next 6,000 years, or for the whole of the Second and Third Ages, there were no recorded volcanic eruptions. Hobbits would have felt the tremors surely and as far as we know there were none recorded in the Shire – unlike the Lonely Mountain and that region of north-west Middle-earth. But, significantly, the Shire is extremely fertile with good soil, which is indicative of volcanic matter being deposited upon the plains by a westerly wind drift beyond the Tower Hills and forming the basis of the agriculture of the next millennia. Could a volcano have erupted once, spectacularly, and then lain dormant for many thousands of years? This cannot be beyond the realms of possibility.

The First Age cataclysm was, in legend, put down to the war between the Hosts of the West and Morgoth. Certainly,

Thangorodrim seems to have been a good candidate for volcanic activity from what the legend tell us of the War of Wrath, and, if it erupted at the same time as Mount Dolmed, it would have caused additional strain on the fault lines surrounding Beleriand. We are told that the lands all down the coast were changed – but how and to what extent is difficult to measure as we do not have tales of any people who lived outside Beleriand in Middle-earth during the First Age.

But what cannot be accounted for is the lack of damage – as far as we are told – to the shores of Valinor and, most especially, Tol Eressëa. Such a huge devastation on the westernmost shores of Middle-earth should have caused massive tidal waves and tsunamis with great destructive potential. In reality, the coasts of Valinor and all the civilisation on the eastern side of the island should have been annihilated. Compare, in real world, the detonation of Thera (now known as Santorini) in the Aegean, in Classical times, when that volcano blew four-fifths of the island out of existence; the tidal waves that swept outwards destroyed the Minoan civilisation on Crete and other surrounding islands. In later times, when Krakatoa blew up near Java, tidal waves affected all areas of the Pacific for thousands of miles around. How could Valinor escape such damage? At this time, it was still within the circles of the world, so presumably, the seas connected it physically to Middle-earth somehow. But what we do not hear of any storms hitting even Tol Eressëa let alone Valinor. Somehow, there was a barrier, either natural or unnatural that acted as a wave-break and dissipated the energy. Unnatural effects would be that Ulmo stood there and held back the wrath of the sea. My theory for a more natural explanation would be to place a great reef – somewhat like the Great Barrier Reef – along the north-south line separating Tol Eressëa from the Great Sea proper. Perhaps this as much as anything prevented anyone sailing west when the two areas were still physically connected.

During the Second Age, Númenóreans visited Middle-earth, living as they did on the westernmost island of the mortal realms, and they reported major features that we can still see on the map of Middle-earth as it was at the end of the Third Age: Umbar and its natural harbour, the mouths of the Anduin which were extremely similar in topography to the Mouths of Sirion in the First Age – and they founded the city of Pelargir up the Anduin. They also explored the Gwathló and cut great swathes of the forests to either side to build their ships. We also know of the presence of the elvish Havens at Mithlond and Harlond on the Gulf of Lune, for Círdan and Gil-galad dwelt there. So the destruction at the end of Second Age can immediately be seen to be on a far smaller scale than those of the end of the First Age.

At the end of the Second Age, Meneltarma in the middle of Númenor blew up in a similar fashion to Krakatoa, destroying the whole island with it in a matter of moments. Upon the waves of the great storm, Elendil and his sons rode out the tidal waves on their nine ships and came to Middle-earth which had had its coastline changed "beyond recognition". Yet, we *do* recognise all the salient features that the Númenóreans mentioned, so how bad was the damage? That there was major storm damage is certain, but it may be that only some headlands were altered, for the rivers did not seem to change their courses nor mountain ranges alter in any way.

At this stage Valinor was sundered from the circles of the world, disassociated with the seas of Middle-earth just before the destruction of Meneltarma – and so, perhaps, shielding the Undying Lands from the close proximity of the Krakatoa-style annihilation of Númenor. So, what was this sundering? The seas are said not to be physically linked any more. Tolkien describes it as being a *less substantial* sea that mariners cross to reach Valinor. Some see the *sundering* process itself as the change from a flat-earth to a round-earth, both symbolically and actually, but of course such a process would be difficult to uphold within a world that Tolkien has tried to ensure is as close to our own as it is possible to sub-create. It *is* our world as far as Tolkien was concerned, but a world far removed from our own in terms of the recorded historical timeline. So flat worlds turning into round spheres is self-evidently not an acceptable physical process – Tolkien after all wrote *The Silmarillion* from 1920 onwards, not circa 1320 when a flat earth might have been acceptable.

I prefer a more radical solution to the sundering problem: that is to look at Valinor as existing within some other dimension of the Universe close to our own but far enough apart to make it very difficult for mortals to reach with their conventional physical means. Yet sometimes it is said that mortals do take the *Straight Road* and reach Valinor, and landing their ships on the golden shores before Taniquetil, they see perfection and then die. The event is a rare one, and mortals are not supposed to be able to reach Valinor without help – remember Frodo departed with help from the three Ringbearers of the Elven Rings, and in token of his right to passage, he bore the jewel that Arwen had given to him. The light of the Blessed Realm is too bright for mortals to live long – it seems an excess of energy burns them out in some way.

Was that all that happened in terms of sea damage to Middle-earth? No, for in circa 1,000 of the Third Age, one of the Gondorian Kings was lost at sea with his ships – and during these same storms much damage was done to the shores of Middle-earth. During that time the Istari were said to have arrived on the shores of Middle-earth. Did they have anything to do with the storms? Very possibly. We know by the end of the Third Age that ships may sail out to Valinor by the *Straight Road*, but none ever return. Perhaps the attempt to send three ships with a wizard aboard each one from Valinor to Middle-earth caused such a rift in the dimensions that there was massive oceanic turbulence that caused gigantic waves to form, and hence the very severe storms. So the arrival of the Istari may well have caused the storms that hit Middle-earth.

It is perhaps because of this consequence that no others have dared return in this way to Middle-earth – Glorfindel presumably was reborn in a new body when he came into *The Lord of the Rings* tale. Those who had departed Valinor were said to be "beyond time and history".

This leads us to the very interesting hypothesis that perhaps the two dimensional planes of Valinor & Tol Eressëa and Middle-earth were drifting ever wider apart from the First Age onwards, and that the energy step was made in travelling towards Valinor. So that each time someone tried to come the other way there was an energy payback, and as time went by that grew greater and greater, until the Wise would realise that the world itself would be endangered by any physical breaking of the barrier if one crossed from Valinor back to Middle-earth.

This would neatly parallel the state of electrons as described by Quantum Physics. An electron may sit in a stable state at one energy level (the equivalent of a being living in Middle-earth in this example). Upon gaining energy, either slowly or in one go, it jumps up into a higher energy orbit which is also stable (the equivalent of a being going from Middle-earth to Valinor). However, should the electron drop back to the lower level, energy must be lost, usually in the form of light, so preserving the third law of thermodynamics:

> matter nor energy can neither be created nor destroyed but merely changed from one form to another.

In the case of a wizard leaving Valinor to land upon the shores of Middle-earth there would also be an energy payback, but in this case the energy comes in the form of great tidal waves and winds, leading to ferocious storms. The energy equation is preserved.

That some form of energy is intimately involved with beings in Middle-earth can most eloquently be demonstrated by the last thing that Frodo sees before he faints and falls from Glorfindel's horse at the Ford of Bruinen: a shining being emanating light. Gandalf explains to him at Rivendell, where he is recovering, that that is how Glorfindel appears "on the other side" – the most direct reference I can find in *The Lord of the Rings* to a parallel dimension. Thus, the two energy states exist side by side both in Middle-earth and Valinor, but the natural state in Middle-earth is the lower energy level, and in Valinor it is the higher. These states are getting further apart, making it more and more difficult for beings from Middle-earth to go to Valinor, and more and more dangerous for those in Valinor to attempt the reverse journey.

At the end of the Third Age, there is no major storm or refashioning of the shoreline of Middle-earth. Instead we have the destruction of Mount Doom, the key volcanic eruption that signals the end of the Age, much as Meneltarma and Mount

Dolmed with Thangorodrim signalled the end of the Second and First Ages.

I hope that this small study might shed some light upon the nature of the relationship between Valinor and Middle-earth, and how the Great Sea connected the two.

Searching for an Earthly Paradise: Some Common Images in the Works of J.R.R. Tolkien and C.S. Lewis

Maria B. Kuteeva

Mythopoeia and Scholarship

The practice of mythopoeia was common to the Inklings, yet the actual approach to creative writing varied. Thus Tolkien's work reflects his scholarly background of an Anglo-Saxon philologist: his Middle-earth is a product of the texts and literary techniques he studied. Tolkien belonged to a philosophical tradition which tried to recreate the lost literatures of the dead languages.[1] Being a perfectionist, he spent years re-writing the same material over and over again. It is therefore little wonder that Tolkien disliked Lewis's Narnia books for their careless attitude to the idea of sub-creation, the matter of language (everybody speaks English), and eclecticism in the use of images:

> "the story was borrowed so indiscriminately from other mythologies and narratives (fauns, nymphs, Father Christmas, talking animals, anything that seemed useful for the plot) that

1. In this connection see particularly Shippey 1992.

43

for Tolkien the suspension of disbelief, the entering into a secondary world, was simply impossible. It just *wouldn't* 'do', and he turned his back on it." (Carpenter 1978, p. 224)

If the same criteria of judgment are applied to the Narnia books as to Tolkien's works, the result is indeed disappointing. However, it is not the same if one's look at Lewis's works taking into account the specific details of his own understanding of writing and literature. Moreover, one also discovers a great deal of Tolkien's influence upon the Narnian *Chronicles*. There are certain characteristics which are, in a sense, close to Tolkien's 'Anglophilia' and his concern about the Machine. Although Lewis's scholarly studies were particularly focused on the Middle Ages and Renaissance, his general understanding of 'periods' in literature was much wider. It implied only one major division: the invention of the Machine in the nineteenth century.[2] Everything before that event he considered to belong to what he called 'Old Western Culture', so that his own specific area was only "a specimen of something far larger, something which had already begun when the *Iliad* was composed and was still almost unimpaired when Waterloo was fought" (Lewis 1969, p. 11).

In the *Chronicles of Narnia* Lewis uses such a wide spectrum of various literary sources, so that he is accused of eclecticism. Lewis was much more interested in 'literature' than Tolkien, and the repertoire of his reading was more wide-ranging than his friend's. One can argue that in his technique of re-writing what had been written previously, Lewis adopted

2. See his inaugural lecture "*De Descriptione Temporum*" reprinted in Selected Literary Essays, ed. Walter Hooper, (London: Geoffrey Bless), 1969.

the 'bookish culture' of the period he studied. Using his own comment on the mediaeval approach to literature, we can say that Lewis wrote about his images not "because his own poetic imagination invented them … but because he has read about them in a book" (Lewis 1966, p. 42).

In his imaginary world Lewis as a 'sub-creator' has "rearranged" elements that we have been given by God, "recombining elements made by Him and already containing His meanings. Because of those divine meanings in our materials it is impossible that we should ever know the whole meaning of our own works." (Lewis 1966 [*Letters*], p. 203). It is interesting to notice that Lewis was also putting into play the elements given by the Creator through the medium of other 'sub-creators', in other words, those present in literature. A very important aspect, therefore, is the use of the literary tradition in the stories.

There are certain guides for the most likely material. Lewis was the central figure of the Inklings, an informal group of writers and academics who used to meet at his rooms at Magdalen College to read and discuss their literary work in progress.[3] But what were the Inklings' meetings apart from *viva voce* readings? Almost all members belonged to the academic world, and their work in progress would not be limited to creative writing. For Tolkien and Lewis, the study of old texts was part of everyday routine. The analysis of sources, in turn, appears as one of the essential methods for mediaevalists and philologists.[4] Thus some manuscripts have not survived in their

3. Short biographical notes on the members of the Inklings can be found in Carpenter 1978, pp. 255-259.
4. An interesting analysis of the utility of source study is given by Katherine O'Brien O'Keeffe 1994. She particularly mentions its use for Anglo-

entirety, and similar motifs recur in different works with certain variations. I am inclined to think that this question emerged during the Inklings' discussions. In other words, the scholarly search for vanished sources nourished the participants' imagination and played its part in mythopoeia.

Unfortunately, apart from occasional remarks in private letters and diaries of the participants, there are no systematic records concerning the Inklings meetings. Yet more food for thought has been provided by the drafts of J.R.R. Tolkien's "The Notion Club Papers".[5] The book was started around the end of 1945, but abandoned and never completed. Although the events take place at Oxford in the future, the years 1986-87, the material which has survived suggests that the work was inspired by the Inklings meetings. "The Papers" are essentially "an elaborate minute book of a club, devoted to conversation, debate, and the discussion of 'papers', in verse or prose, written and read by its members" (NCP Foreword, p. 2).

Part One records the discussion dedicated to the use of the machine in space-travel romance and the problem of dreams as a means of communication with other realities. The first page of one of the manuscript begins thus:

Beyond Lewis

or

Out of the Talkative Planet

Saxonists, including Tolkien (pp. 52-53).
5. First published in J.R.R. Tolkien, *Sauron Defeated: The End of the Third Age* (*The History of the Lord of the Rings, Part Four*), edited by Christopher Tolkien (London: HarperCollins, 1992), pp. 145-331. Later references are given in the main text.

Being a fragment of an apocryphal Inklings' Saga, made by some imitator at some time in the 1980s.[6]

Part Two is largely devoted to Númenor, Tolkien's chief interest. Yet it also discusses the matter of language and myth which was an important concern for the Inklings. Although there is no one-to-one identification of members of the Notion Club with members of the Inklings, one can recognise some of Lewis's characteristics in the portrait and remarks of Philip Frankley. According to Christopher Tolkien's comments on manuscript A, "*Franks* (only becoming *Frankley* in the third text C) is here Lewis, I suppose that my father felt that the name was appropriate for the character" (p. 150). In the second text Frankley, as well as some other members, is also attributed "a taste for romances of travel and time" (p. 151). Eventually, Frankley appears in the MS as a poet, who "suffers from *horror borealis* (as he calls it) and is intolerant of all things Northern and Germanic" (p. 159), a reversal of Lewis's 'Northernness'.[7] In addition, it is also noteworthy that there are some references and assessment of the works of the Inklings by their imaginary 'successors'.

In other words, "The Notion Club Papers" can be helpful for those interested in finding out the sources of the Inklings'

6. p.148. Cf. *Out of the Silent Planet* (1938). In another manuscript of the 'Papers' we come across *Beyond Probability*. In fact, both titles (*Beyond Probability* and *Beyond Lewis*) are a pun on Lewis's *Beyond Personality* (1944). *Probability* alludes to *Personality* in the word appearance, and *Lewis* thus appears as a perfect example of 'personality'. For more discussion see Christopher Tolkien's comments on pp. 148-49.
7. The origins of Lewis's and Tolkien's friendship lay in their shared 'Northernness', the romances of William Morris and interest in mythology. For more details see Lewis's *Surprised by Joy*, 1955, pp. 204-5, and Green & Hooper 1974, p. 93.

works. We shall back this point in due course. Besides, the task of finding the origins becomes easier if words are taken for guides. Thus, Lewis took the name Puddleglum, the famous Marsh-wiggle (*The Silver Chair* (1953)), from Studley's translation of *Tacitae Stygis* in Euripides's *Hippolytus*, 1. 625 as "Stygian puddle glum",[8] Tolkien's *woses* is a derivation from *wodwos* in *Sir Gawain and the Green Knight*, 1. 721 (the word later used by Lewis as *Wooses* in *The Lion, the Witch and the Wardrobe* (1950)); Lewis's Roonwit the Centaur (*Prince Caspian* (1951)) is a reminiscence of Old English *runwita*, knower-of-secrets (*Beowulf*, 1. 1325). Such links with Tolkien are numerous, and they are discussed in more detail elsewhere.[9] There are certain motifs that seem to be particularly attractive for Tolkien and Lewis, such as a dragon lying on treasure, the magical rings that give the power over the World, stone giants (ettens), werewolves, and others. Thus the analysis of literary sources studied by the two scholars can shed more light upon the origins of their own mythopoeia.

The Legend of Saint Brendan

Among the texts possibly discussed by the Inklings, one legend appears to be notable, namely the voyage of Saint Brendan to the Promised Land. What makes one suggest this particular source? Tolkien wrote a poem "Imram" published in 1955.[10]

---

8. Lewis discussed this awkward translation in his *English Literature in the Sixteenth Century*, 1954, p. 256.
9. I am very grateful to Prof. T.A. Shippey, St. Louis University, for his advice in the area of Anglo-Saxon and mediaeval studies. See his *Road* 1992 for more details on the origins of Tolkien's names. On Lewis see also Ford 1980.
10. *Time and Tide* (London) Vol. XXXVI No. 49, 3 December 1955, p. 1561.

A great deal of work went into this poem, with its elaborate versification", writes Christopher Tolkien (NCP, p. 295). Before 1955 the poem had appeared in the manuscript of "The Notion Club Papers" as "The Ballad of Saint Brendan's Death" and "The Death of Saint Brendan".

The mediaeval story of Saint Brendan exists in several versions which shall be discussed shortly. These versions vary in certain episodes, and this obscurity may have served as fecund soil for poetic imagination at different periods. Thus Dante's *Divine Comedy* shows certain signs of the influence of this legend. In the nineteenth century the story of St Brendan inspired Matthew Arnold ("Saint Brendan" (1860)) and Tennyson ("The Voyage of Maeldune, founded on an Irish legend AD 700" (1892)).[11]

What are the primary sources of this legend? Saint Brendan (489-between 570 and 583) was an Irish priest. As with many other early Irish saints, the circumstances surrounding his sanctification are obscure. Brendan's legendary biography is more detailed and colourful than the factual one. Although the core of his legend remains Celtic, scholars also admit the influence of Classical and biblical literatures (Short & Marrilees 1979, p. 2).

Although there were earlier forms of Saint Brendan's legend, they were not preserved until the ninth century. There are two principal texts recounting Brendan's life and travels, each in several versions. They are the *Vita sancti Brendani* and the *Navigatio sancti Brendani*, both prose Latin texts. The first one comprises the stories of two voyages as well as

---

11. Matthew Arnold, *Poetical Works* (London, 1892), pp. 165-67; Tennyson, Works (London, 1892) pp. 529-532.

details of Brendan's ancestry and life until his last moment. The *Navigatio*, is quite different from the *Vita*, being the story of a single seven-year voyage, with the briefest references to the rest of Brendan's life. Scholars suggest a wide range of sources for this work, and also admit that its form is very close to the Irish *immram* ('rowing about') or voyage-tale, a genre in which a sea journey provides the framework for a succession of isolated adventures.[12] The description of the lands visited by the voyagers normally owe much more to imagination than to observation. The *Navigatio* was very popular during the Middle Ages, and the 120 surviving Latin manuscripts are the best proof of that. Moreover, there are several translations and adaptations into the mediaeval vernaculars. The best known of the latter if Benedeit's Voyage of Brendan composed in Anglo-Norman dialect.

Certainly, the *Navigatio* was much more than a voyage tale: it synthesises the Irish myths of a 'happy other world' in the western ocean and Christian visions of heaven and hell. The mediaeval poet Benedeit increases the metaphorical meaning of the journey by making certain changes to the *Navigatio*. He bases his version on a different motif. In his *Voyage of St Brendan* the series of adventures becomes a series of trials. Here the tale acquires a deeper significance than in the Latin version: "From a mere odyssey it becomes a pilgrim's progress, in which the pilgrims pass through a graduated series of trials to taste eventually the joys of paradise" (Waters 1928, p. civ).

Returning to "The Notion Club Papers", we notice that it is

---

12. There are three principle *immrama* that have survived: *The Voyage of Mael Duin*, *The Voyage of Snédgus and Mac Riagla*, and *The Voyage of Hui*, ed. and trans. Whitley strokes, *Revue Celtique* 9 (1888), 447-95, 14-25; 14 (1893), 22-69.

Frankley (originally C.S. Lewis, as has been suggested) who reads the poem to the Club (NCP Night 69:11). In Tolkien's "The Death of Saint Brendan" a younger monk asks Brendan about the most important things that he saw during his journey, so the Saint replies:

> The things I have seen, the many things,
>   have long now faded far;
> only three come clear now back to me:
>   a Cloud, a Tree, a Star. (1. 21-24)

Then Brendan recounts the adventures that happened to his boat, which Tolkien based on legendary material. In Tolkien's version the symbolism of the narrative is renewed, since Frankley has given the Cloud, the Tree and the Star "a twist" that was not in the source. The poem came to Frankley's mind unexpectedly, as a revelation:

> '…I woke up about four days ago with the thing largely fixed, and the name Brendan running in my head… The pictures were quite clear for a while. I read the *Navigatio Sancti Brendani*, of course, once upon a time, years ago, as well as early that Anglo-French thing, Benedeit's *Vita*. But I've not looked at them again – though perhaps if I did, I might find them less disappointing than I remember them.
> … 'And that bit about the "round world" and the "old road",' said Jeremy, 'where did you get that from?'
> 'I don't know,' said Frankley. 'It came in the writing. I got a fleeting picture, but it's faded now.' (NCP Night 69:15-19)

There are two important things to be noticed from this passage. First, the images are created unconsciously on the basis of previous *reading*. Second, they come to Frankley as *pictures* (the word mentioned here twice). This is exactly how Lewis himself describes the origins of his imaginative writing: "All my seven Narnian books, and my three science-fiction books, began with seeing pictures in my head" (Lewis 1966 [*OOW*], p. 42).[13] Also, as we shall see, the three symbolic episodes – a Cloud, a Tree and a Star – have a recognisable correlative in Lewis's story. This would be a remarkable coincidence. By looking at the earlier version from "The Notion Club Papers" (circa 1945) we can find out how Tolkien 'foresees' certain images that will occur in Lewis's *The Voyage of the Dawn Treader* written in 1950.

C.S. Lewis's *The Voyage of the Dawn Treader* in Relationship to Tolkien's Images

Let us now look more closely at the origins of *The Voyage of the Dawn Treader*. First, metaphorically the story is reminiscent of a mediaeval journey with its strong spiritual implication. Thus the children join Caspian in his search for the seven lords, and sail towards the World's End. They pass three Lone Islands, Dragon Island, the Island of Voices, the Dark Island, and, finally, arrive at the End of the World. Each of these stages has its particular sacred meaning, and becomes a profound spiritual experience for King Caspian and the children. In this regard, *The Voyage* is close to Benedeit's *Vita*. However, there are many other literary allusions occurring in the course of the narrative, and most of them reveal connections between the

13. "It all Began with a Picture…" was first published in *Radio Times, Junior Radio Times*, CXLVIII (15 July 1960).

images of Lewis and Tolkien.

The events on Dragon Island evoke the first parallel. The motifs of a hidden treasure and Eustace's metamorphosis into a dragon represent the central idea of the episode. The use of a dragon as a monster and a symbol of greed in literature can be traced far back: "… the dragon that preserves buried treasure (as in *Beowulf*, or the Volsung story) is at least as old as the gold-guarding griffin of the Roman fabulist Phaedrus" (Lewis 1964, p. 23). Lewis's dragon certainly has its origins in the author's 'Northernness' and Tolkien's influence. Its worm-like mighty appearance reminds us of Fáfnir from *Völsunga* saga, by which Lewis was fascinated in his childhood. Fáfnir was not a dragon by birth: once a man, he kills his father in order to possess his treasure, and turns into a terrible dragon for his greed. He lies on his treasures until Sigurd comes to slay him (chapters 14-15). Since Eustace has read "only the wrong books" (Lewis 1952, p. 82), he is not aware what one should expect to find in a dragon's lair, and what is suspicious about the treasure. So, overwhelmed by the precious things he finds, he turns into a dragon whilst asleep.

This idea of turning into a dragon by lying down on hoarded treasure does not occur in any major literary work. However, one can find it amongst the sources of Beowulf, first brought into attention by R.W. Chambers in his *Beowulf: An Introduction*:[14]

Long ago Olrik, in *Dania*, called attention to the likeness between the story of Beowulf's dragon and that of the dragons

---

14. Tolkien refers to Chambers in his Sir Israel Gollancz Memorial Lecture "*Beowulf*: The Monsters and the Critics" read to the British Academy in 1935. The third edition of Chamber's *Beowulf: An Introduction* was supplemented by C.L. Wrenn, who was also a member of the Inklings.

dwelling behind the waterfall in the *Gull-Thoris* saga. These dragons were originally Vikings – Val and his sons: but to save their treasure they had gone behind the waterfall where they lived in the form of flying dragons, lying on their gold, with helmet on head and swords beneath their shoulders. (… And Val also had captured the gold which, as a dragon, he later guarded in the water-cave, from a *jötunn* [giant] who originally dwelt there.) (Chambers 1959, p. 458)

Dragons had been feeding Tolkien's imagination since childhood when he first tried to write a story about a dragon: "My mother said nothing about the dragon, but pointed out that one could not say 'a great green dragon'. I wondered why, and I still do" (L 163:11). Thus later he kept on re-working the motif not only in such popular works as *The Hobbit* (1937) or *Farmer Giles of Ham* (1949) but also in his poetry. Thus there are three versions of a poem dedicated to the motif of Elven treasure and a dragon: two entitled "Iúmonna Gold Galdre Bewunden" (1923 and 1937) and the third "The Hoard" (1962). It is most likely that Tolkien discussed the motif and its allegorical meaning with Lewis.

In the episode of Dragon Island, Lewis combines the use of the literary tradition with a parable, giving the metamorphosis a strong moral implication. Lewis and Tolkien demonstrate close agreement about the connection between avarice and dragon-ness. This theme had been running through since the earliest stages of Tolkien's work, and 'passed on' to Lewis.[15] On the other hand, as T.A. Shippey claims, "the transformation points to the shared belief of the Oxford Inklings that modern civilisation had gone astray through a fascination with metal,

---

15. Cf. *Morgoth's Ring*, p. 400, about the evil inclination in gold.

whether riches or machines" (Shippey 1983, p. 252).

Having passed Dragon Island, the crew of the *Dawn Treader* are tested by a monster, suddenly emerging from the sea. This is the great Sea-Serpent: "… an appalling head reared itself out of the sea. It was all greens and vermilions with purple blotches … and shaped rather like a horse's" (Lewis 1952, p. 108). Reepicheep fights against it. This monster is impossible for the crew to kill, but it, nevertheless, rather stupid. It breaks down the ship's stern, and leaves it with "idiotic satisfaction" on its face (ibid, p. 112). The same kind of monster attacks the monks in Benedeit's *Saint Brendan* (I. 897-968). If in the Latin version it is a fish of great size, in the Anglo-Norman it is definitely called a sea-serpent *marins serpenz* (I. 909), and is vividly described as a monster with fiery breath, bull-like bellowings and fearsome teeth (I. 910-918).

The events on the Island of Voices represent one of the most interesting episodes in Lewis's story. The idea of an apparently uninhabited, but beautifully kept land, comparable with "the grounds of a great English house where ten gardeners were kept" (p. 121), and where during a great feast food and dishes are moving themselves on the table, is reminiscent of the myth of Cupid and Psyche or the Beauty and the Beast. However, this episode also echoes the description of the uninhabited city which the monks of Saint Brendan visit during the beginning of their journey (I. 265-306). Both Latin and Anglo-Norman versions tell about the wonders that they come across there. The latter poem, however, contains more descriptions of marvellous palaces and emphasises that no human is visible in the city (I. 278).

Moreover, here one can observe the whole polyphony of different sources in Lewis's images. Encounters with the inhabitants of remote lands and the descriptions of different sorts of creatures used to be a popular theme of travel literature from the ancient times to the great geographical discoveries of the Renaissance. The invisible inhabitants of Lewis's island turn out to be the Duffers, or Monopods as Lucy calls them. When they eventually become visible, we learn how they rest

> "lying flat on their backs each with its single leg straight up in the air ands its enormous foot spread out about it. ...for the foot kept off both rain and the sun and for a Monopod to lie under its own foot is almost as good as being in a tent" (p. 153).

Where do these creatures come from? As we have already noticed, this image has a variety of sources. Thus Martha Sammons sees the origin in a *skiapod* depicted in *The Bestiary* of the thirteenth century as a creature who "possesses one foot which it uses as a sunshade when lying on its back" (Summons 1979, p. 146). It also reminds us of the description of the Ethiopians in *Travels* by John Mandeville: "In þat contree ben folk þat han but o foot; and þei gon so blyue þat it is meruaylle; and the foot is so large þat it schadoweth all the body a en sonne, whanne þei wole lye and reste hem" (Sisam 1979, p. 96). Lewis first came across the works of Mandeville in adolescence, as he mentions in his autobiography *Surprised by Joy* (Lewis 1955, p. 140). Mandeville may have been one of those whose approach Lewis adopted in his own writing. Thus they both were drawing their description on the basis of previously written works: "… there is so little trace of original observation that it is doubtful whether the author travelled far beyond his library" (Sisam 1979, p. 95).

Mandeville's *Travels* were also an important text for

Tolkien. Thus at the beginning of his academic career Tolkien compiled *A Middle English Vocabulary* (1921) which was included as a glossary in Sisam's *Fourteenth Century Verse and Prose* (1921), containing an extract from Mandeville's *Travels*. In addition, this is "one of the only two non-Biblical works mentioned by the *Gawain* poet, whom T[olkien] spent so much time editing".[16] Such mediaeval works also recur in the scholarly literature on the mediaeval period which the Inklings must have read and known.

In Tolkien's poem about Saint Brendan "a Cloud, a Tree, a Star" appear as the most significant images recalled by the Saint. The 'Cloud' episode runs in the earlier version as follows:

> We sailed for a year and a day and hailed
>   no field nor coast of men;
> no boat nor bird saw we ever afloat
>   for forty days and ten.
> We saw no sun at set or dawn,
>   but a dun cold lay ahead,
> and a drumming there was like thunder coming
>   and a gleam of fiery red.
> ("The Death of Saint Brendan", (I. 25-32); cf. "Imram" (I. 25-32))

This brings us to the next parallel with Lewis's *Voyage*. Having set off from the Island of Voices, the *Dawn Treader* makes her way eastwards. Several days after they find themselves in the mist of endless darkness where one loses the sense of time and direction. The ship stars moving around,

---

16. T.A. Shippey, from a letter to the author, 24 August 1995. In "Purity" the *Gawain* poet used Mandeville's accounts of the palace of the Great Chan and amplify his description of Belshazzar's palace and feast (1439-88) based on Daniel. 5. See Spearing 1970, pp. 16-17, 55, 63.

and there seems to be no way back. From a wild-looking man exhausted by infinite fears the crew learns that in this place one's dreams come true, which shortly becomes the realm of terrifying nightmares. A similar obstacle occurs during Saint Brendan's journey, when his ship runs into thick cloud from which the mariners only escape on the fourth day: "Nües grandes tenerge funt, / ... / Li granz calins tant aorbet, / Qui I entret, tuz asorbet" [great clouds darkness make, / ... / the fog blinds so much / whoever enters there loses sight] (I. 1647-1650). It is noteworthy that this episode occurs just before Saint Brendan's boat enters the Paradise.

Likewise, the Dark Island turns out to be the last serious trial before the World's End. From the beginning of chapter 13 until the end of the book (which coincidences with that of the World) the tone of the narration increasingly becomes higher and more mysterious. What the adventurers find on the last island, the beginning of the World's End, has certain parallels with the tradition associated with the story of the Holy Grail, the vessel of the Last Supper filled with Christ's blood and kept by Joseph of Arimathea in the centre of the altar. In Lewis's story it is a mystic table, full of various gorgeous meals, which is renewed every day; the table itself was set by the bidding of Aslan. The food on the table is renewed by numerous birds, falling down as "heavy snow" (p. 186). This is reminiscent of the dove of the Holy Spirit, or the biblical manna which the Lord "rains" from heaven to feed the Israelites in the desert (Exodus, 16:4), and the ravens feeding Elijah with bread and flesh every morning and evening (I Kings, 17:6). At the same time, the theme of the Paradise of Birds appears three times during the voyage of Saint Brendan (section 10 in *Navigatio*; lines 489-578, 867-883, 1623-1628 in Benedeit) when monks come across the tree covered with white birds, one of which speaks to Saint Brendan the words of God. Benedeit's tree is "blanche cume marbre, / E les fruiles mult sunt ledes, / De ruge e blanc taceledes [as white as marble with wide leaves speckled with red and white]" (I. 490-92). It is great and strong, stretching up into the cloud. This image leads us to Tolkien's tree:

> so wide its branches, the least could hide
>   in shade an acre long,
> and they rose as steep as mountain-snows
>   those boughs so broad and strong;
> for white as a winter to my sight
>   the leaves of that tree were,
> they grew more close than swan-wing plumes,
>   all long and soft and fair.
> ("Death of Saint Brendan" (I. 77-84); cf. "Imram" (I. 67-76))

At the End of the World the final theme of "a Star" is introduced. The voyagers of the *Dawn Treader* meet Ramandu, a retired star. "His silver beard came down to his bare feet in front and his silver hair hung down to his heels behind and his robe appeared to be made from the fleece of silver sheep... the air became full of voices – voices which took up the same song that the Lady and her Father were singing, but in far wilder tones and in a language which no one knew" (p. 185-86). Again, this evokes Tolkien's lines:

> From the sky came dropping down on high
>   a music not of bird,
> not voice of man, nor angel's voice;
>   but maybe there is a third

fair kindred in the world yet lingers
  beyond the foundered land.
("Death of Saint Brendan" (I. 97-102); cf. "Imram" (I. 89-94))

Lewis's controversy with the contemporary view on nature and the Universe found its expression in the dialogue between Eustace and Ramandu:

> 'I am a star at rest, …' answered Ramandu…
> 'In our world,' said Eustace, 'a star is a huge ball of flaming gas.'
> 'Even in your world, my son, that is not what a star is but only what it is made of.' (p. 189)

Ramandu's last statement is a clear reminiscence of the memorable talk with Tolkien about myth, when Lewis himself was taking Eustace's position, saying that "myths are lies, even though lies breathed through silver" (Carpenter 1987, p. 151).[17] Now he is mocking himself, using the images from the poem "Mythopoeia" which he received from Tolkien after their talk:

> You look at trees and label them just so,
> (for trees are 'trees', and growing is 'to grow');
> you walk the earth and tread with solemn pace
> one of the many minor globes of Space:
> a star's a star, some matter in a ball
> compelled to courses mathematical
> amid the regimented, cold, Inane,
> where destined atoms are each moment slain…
>
> He sees no stars who does not see them first
> of living silver made that sudden burst

---

17. This controversy is described in Carpenter 1987, pp. 150-51; and Carpenter 1978, pp. 42-45.

to flame like flowers beneath the ancient song,
whose very echo after-music long has since pursued.[18]

In the finale of the story, just like Saint Brendan's boat, the *Dawn Treader* sails further to the End of the World. Lewis puts his own thoughts in Edmund's mouth: "There is nothing particularly exciting about a round world when you're there" (p. 208). Narnia is finite – "the World like a great round table and the waters of all the oceans endlessly pouring over the edge" (p. 207). Thus here we can observe another parallel in the Inklings' understanding of imaginary worlds: in Norse mythology the world is conceived as a circular disk, in the middle of which there is a circular portion, *Miðgarð* ('the middle enclosure'), where men dwell.[19] This was the source for Middle-earth, as Tolkien himself pointed out in his "Guide to the Names in *The Lord of the Rings*".[20]

The Narnian Paradise is the Utter East, a traditional mediaeval concept (Lewis 1964, p. 144). Everything changes when the *Dawn Treader* enters the Last Sea: one needs no sleep, no food, the sun becomes several times its normal size, the water is very clear and sweet. The idea of an Earthly Paradise beyond the sea was also a permanent source of fascination for Tolkien. "The longing for a Paradise on Earth, a paradise of natural beauty, was compelling and repeated and there before Tolkien took to fiction." (Shippey 1992, p. 252). Unlike Lewis, he would associate its location with the Western Ocean. As

18. "Mythopoeia" in Tolkien, *Tree and Leaf*, pp. 97-98.
19. The diagram illustrating Norse cosmology is given in E.V. Gordon, A.R. Taylor n.d., p. 196. E.V. Gordon was a good friend and colleague of Tolkien during his work at Leeds (1920-1925).
20. Cf. entries on Middle-earth and Isengard. See Lobdell 1975, pp. 187, 189.

early as 1927 Tolkien published a poem called "The Nameless Land", which was later reworked in "The Song of Ælfwine", and is closely connected with "The Notion Club Papers" and the poem "Imram" mentioned above.[21] The poem was written in 1924 "inspired by reading *Pearl* for examination purposes" (Carpenter 1987, p. 107) and showed the influence of mediaeval descriptions of Paradise:

> Such loveliness to look upon
> Nor Bran nor Brendan ever won,
>   Who foam beyond the furthest sea
> Did dare, and dipped behind the sun
>   On winds unearthly wafted free.
> Than Tir-nan-Og more fair and free,
>   Than Paradise more faint and far,
> O! shore beyond the Shadowy Sea,
>   O! land forlorn where lost things are,
> O! mountains where no man may be!
> (I. 44-61)[22]

There is another interesting analogy in the ideas of Lewis and Tolkien. However, close the Dawn Treader approaches Aslan's country, there is no way for anyone to actually enter it: as described by Lewis, the Paradise lies beyond the edge of the world. A similar conception is developed by Tolkien in his "Notion Club Papers".[23] After the Númenórean catastrophe the

---

21. The variants of the poem and further comments one can find in *The Lost Road and Other Writings*, 1987, pp. 98-103.
22. "The Nameless Land" was first published in *Realities: an Anthology of Verse*, ed. G.S. Tancred (Leeds: Swan Press; London: Gay and Hancock, 1927), pp. 24-5.
23. See Night 70 in *Sauron Defeated*, pp. 277-80.

straight road to the land of the immortal in the West disappears, and ever since any attempt to search for it is in vain. This parallel is particularly remarkable because the idea of such 'detached' Earthly Paradise is not typical of ancient sources.[24] Yet one should keep in mind one crucial difference between the imaginary worlds of Lewis and Tolkien: whilst the former was drawing a picture of Narnia, a different world which can be entered by means of magic, the latter was describing an imaginary period of the history of our world. Thus the relationship between the Paradise and our world in the works of the two authors is not exactly the same.[25]

Conclusion

What do all these parallels tell us about? In all likelihood, Tolkien discussed the images of Saint Brendan's legend and other journeys in search of the Earthly Paradise with Lewis, making an impact upon his practice of mythopoeia. *The Voyage of the Dawn Treader* provides the most illustrative example. In this third Narnia book, Lewis manages to combine numerous literary images with various origins into a harmony of narration. The journey represents not only adventure, but the travels and the progress of a soul driven by longings for the divine.

There are close connections between the academic activities

---

24. Many thanks to Anders Stenström for his suggestion of this similarity. He also mentioned that a similar solution was found by Lord Dunsany in his *The King of Elfland's Daughter* (1928).
25. Lewis gave a more detailed description of the Paradise in *The Magician's Nephew* (1956) and *The Last Battle* (1956). It is "world within world, Narnia within Narnia", as Mr Tumnus explains "like an onion: except as you go in and in, each circle is larger than the last" (*The Last Battle*, p. 181).

and imaginative works of Tolkien and Lewis. Their study of medieval texts could not but reflect upon their imaginative works. Therefore, one can claim that the scholarly search for vanished literary sources fostered the authors' imagination and played its part in mythopoeia. And, as argued above, looking at the Inklings' meetings as part of the University's 'informal' academic life can shed more light upon the origins of their creativity. The use of the legend of Saint Brendan serves as a proof of my assertions.

From the beginning to the end of his life, Lewis remained in confrontation with contemporary culture, being misunderstood even amongst his colleagues and friends in the academic world. When in 1954 he eventually became Professor of Medieval and Renaissance English Literature at Cambridge, he entitled his inaugural lecture "*De Descriptione Temporum*". In it, he claims that there is a vast gap lying between modern and Old Western Culture, of which he considered himself a representative: "I myself belong far more to that Old Western order than to yours… I read as a native texts that you must read as foreigners" (Lewis 1969, p. 13). Lewis finished his lecture ironically, "where I fail as a critic, I may still be useful a specimen. I would even dare to go further. Speaking not only for myself but for all other Old Western men whom you may meet, I would say, use your specimens while you can. There are not going to be many more dinosaurs" (p. 14). The definition of an 'Old Western man' has been used by T.A. Shippey in his Preface to the second edition of *The Road to Middle-earth* in reference to Tolkien. As presented by Carpenter, the works of these two academics and writers, particularly at the beginning of their careers, appear to be very different (Carpenter 1978, pp. 22-25), and they probably were in their lifetime. Today we have far more chances to see similarities in the work of those who have become to be regarded by the modern world as 'old-fashioned'. Yet for many of us such 'old-fashionedness' does not bare any negative connotation. Today the works of both Tolkien and Lewis can be regarded as part of the eternal realm of Myth.

Bibliography

Carpenter, Humphrey, *Tolkien: A Biography* (London: Allen & Unwin, 1987 (orig. 1977)).
---, *The Inklings: C.S. Lewis, J.R.R. Tolkien, Charles Williams and their friends* (London: Allen & Unwin, 1978).
--- (ed.), *Letters of J.R.R. Tolkien* (London: Allen & Unwin, 1981).

Chambers, R.W., *Beowulf: An Introduction to the Study of the Poem with a Discussion of the Stories of Offa and Finn,* with a supplement by C.L. Wrenn, 3rd edition (Cambridge: University Press, 1959).

Ford, Paul F., *Companion to Narnia* (San Francisco: Harper & Row, 1980).

Gordon, E.V., A.R. Taylor, *Introduction to Old Norse*, 2nd revised edition (Oxford: Clarendon Press, n.d.), p.196.

Green, Roger Lancelyn, and Walter Hooper, *C.S. Lewis: A Biography* (London: William Collins, 1974).

Lewis, C.S., *The Voyage of the Dawn Treader* (London: Geoffrey Bles, 1952).
---, *English Literature in the Sixteenth Century, excluding Drama (The Oxford History of English Literature*, Vol. III) (Oxford: Clarendon Press, 1954).
---, *Surprised by Joy: the shape of my early life* (London: Geoffrey Bles, 1955).
---, *The Last Battle* (London: The Bodley Head, 1956).
---, *The Discarded Image: An Introduction to Medieval and Renaissance Literature* (Cambridge: Cambridge University Press, 1964).
---, *Of Other Worlds: Essays and Stories*, edited by Walter Hooper (London: Geoffrey Bles, 1966).

---, *Studies in Medieval and Renaissance Literature*, collected by Walter Hooper (Cambridge: Cambridge University Press, 1966).
---, *Selected Literary Essays*, edited by Walter Hooper (Cambridge: Cambridge University Press, 1969).

Lewis, W.H. (ed.), *Letters of C.S. Lewis* (London: Geoffrey Bles, 1966).

Lobdell, Jared (ed.), *A Tolkien Compass* (La Salle, Illinois: Open Court, 1975).

O'Brien O'Keeffe, Katherine, "Source, method, Theory, practice: on reading two old English verse texts", in *Bulletin of John Rylands University Library*, Vol. 76 (Manchester, 1994) I. 50-72.

Sammons, Martha C., *A Guide through of Narnia* (Hodder & Stoughton, London, Sydney, Auckland, Toronto, 1979).

Shippey, T.A., "The Chronicles of Narnia", in *Survey of Modern Fantasy Literature*, ed. Frank N. Magili (Salim Press: Eaglewood Cliffs, N.J., 1983), pp. 248-255.
---, *The Road to Middle-earth*, 2nd enlarged edition (London: HarperCollins, 1992).

Short, Ian and Brian Merrilees (ed.), Benedeit, *The Anglo-Norman Voyage of St. Brendan*, (Manchester: Manchester University Press, 1979).

Sisam, Kenneth (ed.), *Fourteenth Century Verse and Prose* (Oxford: Clarendon Press, 1970 (orig. 1921)).

Spearing, A.C., *The Gawain-Poet: A Critical Study* (Cambridge: Cambridge University Press, 1970).

Tolkien, J.R.R., "Iúmonna Gold Galdre Bewunden", *The Gryphon, New Series*, Vol. VI No. 4, January (Leeds University, 1923), 130; *The Oxford Magazine*, Vol. LV No. 15, March (Oxford: Oxonian Press, 1937), 473.

---, "The Nameless Land", in *Realities: an Anthology of Verse*, ed. G.S. Tancred (Leeds: Swan Press; London: Gay and Hancock, 1927), pp. 24-5.

---, "*Beowulf.* The Monsters and the Critics", *Proceedings of the British Academy*, XXII (1936).

---, "Imram", *Time and Tide* (London) Vol. XXXVI No. 49, 3 December 1955, p. 1561.

---, "The Hoard", *The Adventures of Tom Bombadil and other verses from the Red Book* (London: Allen & Unwin, 1962).

---, *The Lost Road and Other Writings: Language and Legend before 'The Lord of the Rings'*, edited by Christopher Tolkien (London: Allen & Unwin, 1987).

---, "Mythopoeia", in J.R.R. Tolkien, *Tree and Leaf*, edited by Christopher Tolkien (London: Allen & Unwin, 1988).

---, *Sauron Defeated: The End of the Third Age (The History of the Lord of the Rings, Part Four)*, edited by Christopher Tolkien (London: HarperCollins, 1992).

---, *Morgoth's Ring (The History of Middle-earth, Part Ten)*, edited by Christopher Tolkien (London: HarperCollins, 1993).

Waters, E.G.R. (ed.), *The Anglo-Norman Voyage of St. Brendan by Benedeit* (Oxford: Clarendon Press, 1928).

The Sea-Bell: A Voyage of Exploration

Christine Davidson

One must be aware (when one thinks about it) of how important a part is played by the sea in Tolkien's writings. From the playful tricks of Fastitocalon to the constant underlying theme of a sea-longing in *The Lord of the Rings*, the fascination of the sea is never far away; a fascination that calls to the child in all of us, standing at the edge of a sandy beach to gaze in wonder at that mysterious expanse of water, longing to learn what unimagined lands may lie on the other side.

One piece that has made a profound impression on me is "The Sea-bell", the last but one, rather anomalous poem in the collection *The Adventures of Tom Bombadil*. Tolkien himself remarks on this in his introductory explanation:

> "...It is the latest piece and belongs to the Fourth Age; but it is included here, because a hand has scrawled at its head "Frodo's Dreme". That is remarkable, and though the piece is most unlikely to have been written by Frodo himself, the title shows that it was associated with the dark and despairing dreams which visited him in March and October during his last three years... The thought of the Sea was ever-present in the background of hobbit imagination; but fear of it and distrust of all Elvish lore, was the prevailing mood in the Shire at the end of the Third Age, and that mood was not entirely dispelled by

the events and changes with which that Age ended." (Tolkien, 1962)

One wonders why the sea should be "ever-present in the background of hobbit imagination", a people that, so far as we are told, had their origins in the middle of a large continent and progressed from a semi-nomadic hunting and gathering way of life to settled agriculture; though, if the poem holds any echo of the truth, the sea was indeed perilous to venture, not only to hobbits, but to any of mortal blood.

I would like to look at this poem in some detail, exploring what it has to say, following the wind, in a sense, to see to what shores it may take us.

> In my fingers shaken I heard waken
>   a ding within, by a harbour bar
> a buoy swinging, a call ringing
>   over endless seas, faint now and far.
> Then I saw a boat silently float
>   on the night-tide, empty and grey.
> 'It is later than late! Why do we wait?'
>   I leapt in and cried: 'Bear me away!'

First the call, awakening latent desire, as the sound of seabirds rouses the heart of an Elf of Middle-earth to restless longing. Then the means: the empty, inviting boat. This is an image that goes back a long way in fantasy and romance. The *Morte D'Arthur* tells of such mysterious boats:

"And on the strand he found a ship covered all with white samite… And as soon as he entered into the ship, the ship departed into the sea, and went so fast that to him seemed the ship went flying, but it was soon dark so that he might know no man, and so he slept till it was day." (Malory, 1969)

This mysterious, magical lure of the sea is still with us, as expressed by John Masefield:

I must go down to the sea again,
  To the lonely sea and the sky,
And all I ask is a tall ship
  And a star to steer her by,
(Masefield, 1902)

But Tolkien's boat, like Malory's, steers a course of its own with the line "It bore me away, wetted with spray" leading to "the hidden teeth of a perilous reef".

This is a sombre counterpoint to the light-hearted voyage of "Errantry" earlier in the collection. Here too the "merry passenger" comes to a deserted isle but instead encounters a river Derrilyn which "goes merrily for ever on".

The rhyme-scheme and alliteration of "The Sea-Bell" are complex, as in "Errantry". But the effect is deeper and darker. "Errantry" bubbles cheerfully along, like the running river Derrilyn. "The Sea-Bell" gives the impression of much longer lines, but in fact where "Errantry" has eight syllables per line – invariably – "The Sea-Bell", though occasional lines are longer, has mainly no more than eight or nine. It is the metre which makes the difference, rather like the contrast in music between a brisk two-four time and the lilting double emphasis of six-eight. The metre of "The Sea-Bell" is far freer, making for a richer weave than the tongue-twisting babble of "Errantry".

Glittering sand slid through my hand,
dust of pearl and jewel-grist,

trumpets of opal, roses of coral,
flutes of green and amethyst.

It would almost seem that the two mariners have come to the same place as the "merry passenger" who also discovers jewels of coral, ivory and emerald. Where is this shore? *The Silmarillion* would suggest that it is in Eldamar, where the Teleri made their abode when at last they came to Aman.

"Many jewels the Noldor gave them, opals and diamonds and pale crystals, which they strewed upon the shores and scattered in the pools; marvellous were the beaches of Elendë in those days." (Tolkien, 1977)

This would bear out the idea that the enchanted boat is Telerin. For it is also said that those "…waters no vessels save those of the Teleri had known."

But the jewels in "The Sea-Bell" mask an underlying menace:

But under cliff-eaves there were glooming caves,
  weed-curtained, dark and grey;
a cold air stirred in my hair,
  and the light waned, as I hurried away.

The whole of the preceding stanza is virtually a description of Keates' "…foam of perilous seas, in faery lands forlorn." (Keates, "Ode to a Nightingale") In that poem also there is a bell, though with opposite effect to that of the Sea-Bell; rather than summon the poet across the perilous sea, it calls him from his romantic reverie back to himself.

In Tolkien's bone-like cliffs and glittering jewels there is also something of Ariel's song in *The Tempest*:

> Of his bones are coral made,
> These are pearls that were his eyes.
> (Shakespeare, 1623)

Here too there is a sea-bell ringing, and the disembodied voices Prospero summons to amaze and bewilder his captives foreshadow those in Tolkien's poem.

But neither Keats nor Shakespeare stay with these magic images for long. They allow a glimpse, then return to the other things they intend the Ode, or the Play, to tell us. Tolkien, in a sense, picks up these fragments, expanding them – I will not say embellishing them, as that implies mere ornamentation – Tolkien expands them into a large image, many faceted and deeply satisfying.

The country the traveller discovers has its roots in European myth. For the Greeks, it was the enchanted garden of the Hesperides that lay at the end of the world. As knowledge of geography increased this moved across the Mediterranean to North Africa finally finishing up somewhere west of the Pillars of Hercules. Hercules himself was believed to have sailed there, in order to perform one of his twelve great labours: he killed a dragon, and stole some of the golden apples that grew there.

Golden apples also figure in the Norse myth of Idun, goddess of youth; and an apple-bough in the Celtic legend of Bran, who set sail for the wondrous Isles of the West.

> There is a distant isle,
> Around which sea-horses glisten…
> Without grief, without sorrow, without death…

The sea washes the wave against the land,
Hair of crystal drops from its mane.
Wealth, treasures of every hue,
Are in Ciuin, a beauty of freshness,
Listening to sweet music,
Drinking the best of wine.
(Ashe, 1990)

Then there is also Arthur's Isle of Avalon – apples again. Were these stories trying to tell our forbears something about the efficacy of Vitamin C? Well, who knows.

In Tolkien's full mythology of course, the golden apples are transformed into the brilliant fruit of the red-gold Tree of Light, Laurelin. But there is no mention of fruit trees in this poem. Here is not a garden at all, but a heightened natural landscape the Lake Poets would have appreciated.

Tolkien's western land is Aman, the Blessed Realm, Valinor, the abode of the godlike Valar. *The Silmarillion* tells that only one voyager was ever permitted to set foot there: Eärendil, of half-elven blood.

Yet it is also said that, after the Fall of Númenor and the bending of the world,

"...tales and rumours arose along the shores of the sea concerning mariners and men forlorn upon the water who, by some fate or grace or favour of the Valar, had entered in upon the Straight Way and had come ...verily to the last beaches on the margin of Aman, and there had looked upon the White Mountain, dreadful and beautiful, before they died." (Tolkien, 1977)

There is no mention in "The Sea-Bell" of the White

Mountain. Perhaps this is not truly Valinor, only one of the Enchanted Isles. Or perhaps this traveller has landed too far from the mountain, or it is obscured, or he does not raise his eyes high enough. The land he discovers is less sublime, its magic lying in smaller, more intrinsically familiar things.

The next verse evokes thoughts of the Elvish feasting in Mirkwood, and Lúthien dancing in Doriath:

I heard dancing there, music in the air,
  feet going quick on the green floors.
But wherever I came, it was ever the same:
  the feet fled, and all was still;
never a greeting, only the fleeting
  pipes, voices, horns on the hill.

The animals, especially the brocks, recall Narnia; and the last line, definitely an echo of Tennyson's "horns of Elfland faintly blowing". (Tennyson, 1850)

Eärendil too found Valinor uninhabited:

He walked in the deserted ways of Tirion, and the dust upon his raiment and shoes was a dust of diamonds... And he called aloud in many tongues, both of Elves and Men, but there was none to answer him.

But Eärendil is eventually summoned to the Halls of the Valar. Even the "merry passenger" of "Errantry" contrives after initial loneliness to snare a butterfly and marry her, although it ends in tears. No doubt the song that conjured the butterfly was as light and nonsensical as "Errantry" itself. In Færie, it seems, one gets precisely what one asks for.

I feel I should make some mention of Bilbo's poem sung

in the House of Elrond (Tolkien, 1954/5), since its theme is also a voyage to Valinor – Eärendil's. However, since the metre is that of "Errantry", the style is quite different to that of "The Sea-Bell", and despite similar elements, such as the perilous voyage and enchanted landfall, the poems have little in common. One place where they come together is the mention of *Evereven*, "where softly silver fountains fall", and a few other images, also shared with "Errantry", as: "Elvenhome the green and fair", "strands of pearl", "yellow gold and jewels wan".

Another poem that seeks to evoke the alien magic of wild places is William Allingham's "The Fairies", once familiar to every schoolchild:

> Up the airy mountain,
> Down the rushy glen,
> We daren't go a-hunting
> For fear of little men.
> (Allingham, 1939)

Within this "childish" poem lie disturbing hints of old dark folklore. The fairies are dangerous, and not to be provoked. Several of the images here are echoed in the later parts of "The Sea-Bell"; there is the old grey king on the hill-top who has "nigh lost his wits", the child stolen for seven years, who dies of sorrow because "her friends have all gone".

> They have kept her ever since
> Deep within the lake,
> On a bed of flag-leaves
> Watching till she wake.
> (Allingham, 1939)

Of river-leaves and the rush-sheaves
I made me a mantle of jewel-green,
a tall wand to hold, and a flag of gold;
my eyes shone like the star-sheen.

Up to now, Tolkien's poem has expressed mystery, enchantment, beauty beyond the everyday, with only hints, as in Allingham's, of a darker side. But now the reversal comes, a reversal precipitated by the traveller himself. For he is not content only to wonder among these marvels to which he has been brought. Unable to communicate with the "voices on the hill", he challenges them:

Why do none speak, wherever I go?
  Here now I stand, king of this land,
with gladdon-sword and reed-mace.
  Answer my call! Come forth all!
Speak to me words! Show me a face!'

Here is Lancelot, mad in the woods because of forbidden love; Thomas the Rymer also, and all the other mortals that grow old in what appears only a brief time in "fair Elfland". Here too is Persephone, summer turned to winter during her imprisonment in the cold domain of the King of the Dead; and even Keat's Knight-at-Arms,

…Alone and palely loitering
When the sedge is withered from the lake
  and no birds sing.

…then I stumbled on;
  like a hunting bat shadow was over me;

77

In my ears dinned a withering wind,
  and with ragged briars I tried to cover me.

But the traveller is not loitering – he is fleeing. As the sea is never still, so this poem, like "Errantry", portrays continuous movement.

My hands were torn and my knees worn,
  and years were heavy upon my back,
when the rain in my face took a salt taste,
  and I smelled the smell of sea-wrack.

Here we have another Ancient Mariner, longing to end his ill-fated voyage and return home.

At last there came light in my long night,
  and I saw my hair hanging grey.
'Bent though I be, I must find the sea!
  I have lost myself, and I know not the way,
but let me be gone!'

There are other reminders too of Coleridge's "Rime of the Ancient Mariner":

Birds came sailing, mewing, wailing;
I heard voices in cold caves,
seals barking, and rock snarling,
and in spout holes the gulping of waves.

The sea in Tolkien's poem, like the land, teems with life. Yet the traveller is as isolated among it as the Ancient Mariner, "alone in a wide, wide sea". Unlike the Ancient Mariner, who kills the albatross, he does no apparent harm to any of it. But the Ancient Mariner begins his atonement with his love for the water-snakes, the only creatures that come near him. Tolkien's traveller, despite his enforced sojourn amid raw nature in the forest, relates to it not at all; his desire to dominate it turns to fear. He is a Hobbit, a would-be tiller of earth and tamer of its beasts, not an Elf who empathises with the wild and free.

In both poems, the mariners encounter conditions that mirror the coldness of their hearts:

> And now there came both mist and snow
> And it was wondrous cold
> And Ice, mast high, came floating by,
> As green as emerald.
> (Coleridge)

> Winter came fast; into a mist I passed,
>   to land's end my years I bore;
> snow was in the air, ice in my hair,
>   darkness was lying on the last shore.

This is the realm of snow and ice feared by the Norsemen, for whom Hell was an arctic, never-ending winter, which brings to mind the crossing of the Noldor across the Helcaraxë where many began to repent of their journey and exile.

The traveller in "The Sea-Bell" has also repented of his journey. But he is luckier than many, if it is indeed Valinor to which he has come. For in *The Silmarillion* we are told:

> "… these isles were strung as a net in the Shadowy Seas… Hardly might any vessel pass between them, for in the dangerous sounds the waves sighed for ever upon dark rocks shrouded in mist." (Tolkien, 1977)

How is it that the traveller has escaped this fate? It might be because hobbits are, as some of the Wise discover, more resilient than other races, more tenacious in their longing for the fields of home. A better explanation would be, I think, that the enchanted boat was indeed Telerin, and brought the traveller, bound in sleep, through the isles to the very shores of Eldamar. Perhaps he was even brought there deliberately, for he did recognise the call of the bell. But if there was a purpose, he could not achieve it. The title "Frodo's Dreme" would bear out this interpretation; shown Elvendom, but unable to become part of it, denied power (when Gollum stripped him of the Ring) and returning home spent and in despair. This is one way, the twisted, tarnished way of black depression, to view the meaning of Frodo's quest.

A further parallel to the "Rime of the Ancient Mariner" is found in the return of the seafarer to his home. This traveller too is feared, shunned, by those he meets. He too, has brought nothing tangible back from his voyage. But he can find no cheerful wedding feast, no listener who will hear his tale. His fate appears to be worse than that of the Ancient Mariner, though his crimes are far less; though the attempt to rule Færie might be seen to stem from a hubris similar to that which prompted the slaying of the albatross. Coleridge's mariner repents his action. Tolkien's does not; despite relating it, he seems unaware of its significance, perhaps incapable of understanding what he has done. A hobbit Ar-Pharazôn, as his might is less, in both wisdom and power, his punishment befits his stature.

> Never will my ear that bell hear,
>   never my feet that shore tread,
> never again, as in sad lane,

in blind alley and in long street
ragged I walk. To myself I talk;
for still they speak not, men that I meet.

What has happened to the traveller? He has heard the call, braved the Sea, but the world he found, though beautiful to wander in, will not accept his all-too-mortal efforts to possess it. He seeks to return, yet though the Blessed Realm has rejected him, his experience has changed him too much for him to fit once more into his own world. The girl in the following, and last, poem ("The Last Ship") avoids this fate: called to go with the Elves, she is tempted, but refuses:

'I cannot come!' they heard her cry.
'I was born Earth's daughter!'

Firiel dreams of Elvenhome, but returns to her mundane work and life. As "The Sea-Bell" shows, such dreams are dangerous to pursue. So no doubt Frodo felt, when weighed down with the Ring's despair. He, of course, was in the end one of the few mortals permitted to attain the Blessed Realm, because of his sacrifice.

What is Tolkien telling us? That to pursue such a dream is doomed to failure? That we may gain the shadow but not the substance, and returning, become strange to our own folk? Perhaps, in the pursuit of his own dream, he at times felt this. Perhaps there is also an echo here of *Leaf by Niggle*, (Tolkien, 1964) where Niggle, after all his striving, can only attain the perfection of his work after death. A common metaphor for death is crossing the river, or leaving harbour to set out across the sea. We may ourselves believe that Tolkien did achieve his own dream in this world, leaving it for us to marvel at.

But we should heed his warning. To leave our own familiar shores may lead us to an empty land, fair with its guiding genius fled. We cannot exist in Valinor, nor yet in Middle-earth. We cannot pursue another's dream. To paraphrase the words of Legolas in Hollin:

> Fair he wrought it, high he builded it;
>   But he is gone. He is gone.
> (Tolkien, 1954/5)

Bibliography

Allingham, William, "The Faeries", in ed. Sir Arthur Quiller-Couch, *The Oxford Book of English Verse*, 1939, Clarendon Press, Oxford.

Ashe, Geoffrey, 1990, *Mythology of the British Isles*, Methuen.

Coleridge, Samuel Taylor, "The Rime of the Ancient Mariner" in ed. W.H. Auden & Norman Holmes Pearson, *Poets of the English Language* Vol II, Ayre & Spottiswoode.

Keats, John, "Ode to a Nightingale", in ed. W.H. Auden & Norman Holmes Pearson, P*oets of the English Language* Vol II, Ayre & Spottiswoode.
---, "La Belle Dame Sans Merci", in in ed. W.H. Auden & Norman Holmes Pearson, *Poets of the English Language* Vol II, Ayre & Spottiswoode.

Malory, Sir Thomas, *Le Morte D'Arthur*, Penguin Classics, Vol II, 1969, Penguin Books.

Masefield, John, 1902, "Sea Fever", in *Oxford Book of 20th Century English Verse*, 1973, Oxford University Press, Oxford.

Shakespeare, William, *The Tempest*, Dent & sons.

Tennyson, Lord Alfred, "The Princess" in *The Poetical Works of Lord Tennyson*, 1850, Collins Clear-type Press.

Tolkien, J.R.R., *The Lord of the Rings*, 1954/5, George, Allen & Unwin, London.
---, *The Adventures of Tom Bombadil*, 1962, George, Allen & Unwin, London.
---, *Tree and Leaf*, 1964, George, Allen & Unwin, London.
---, *The Silmarillion*, 1977, George, Allen & Unwin, London.

Tolkien-on-Sea:
The View from the Shores of Middle-earth

John Ellison

"I do like to be beside the seaside." That traditional time-honoured lay used to typify much of the character of England and the English. It calls up, for those who experienced the reality, memories of the English people on holiday in the days before their habits were radically changed by charter air travel; images of muddy (Weston-Super-Mare), or shingly (Eastbourne) beaches; concerts or entertainments on piers or bandstands; sticks of rock (Blackpool or others), and, of course, seaside boarding houses and their formidable landladies. These traditional pleasures were very much part of Tolkien's own lifestyle, as a glance at the biography by Humphrey Carpenter (Carpenter, 1977), or at John and Priscilla Tolkien's memoir in photographs, *The Tolkien Family Album* (Tolkien & Tolkien, 1992), will confirm.

Note, however, that the song hymns the pleasure of being *beside* the sea, not *on* it. Indeed the expression, "all at sea" signifies something very different. England, Scotland and Wales have always, it is true, been regarded as sea-faring nations *par excellence*, and they like to think of themselves as such. In reality, though only a small minority of their populations have otherwise than in time of war regularly, "gone down to the sea in ships, and carried on their business in great waters". Serious or extensive voyaging has always either been the prerogative of the wealthy, or has fallen to those whose employment or profession required them to travel far overseas. "Messing about in boats", on lakes or rivers is, and has been, the province of most of the ordinary people of this country; and one will recall that even this was too adventurous and dangerous a pastime for the majority of hobbits. The genre of "sea-stories", on the other hand, is a well established one as represented, for instance, by the *Captain Hornblower* series, and has perhaps helped to foster a self-image of the English as natural sailors. Whether it was at all to Tolkien's taste, I don't know. He did make one long sea-voyage in his life, but as he was only three years old at the time it can hardly have represented a formative experience for the rest of his life. His subsequent sea-going experience seems to have been confined to occasional crossings of the English and Irish channels, either in the course of transport in the First World War, or made necessary in the course of holidays in Europe or Ireland. (As anyone who has experienced the old steamer trip from Fishguard to Rosslare could recall – and the Holyhead-Dublin one wasn't all that much more enticing – it was anything but a romantic or life-enhancing sea-going experience). All this was natural enough for Tolkien; having, as he did, a large family to bring up and educate, he didn't have any opportunity of extensive sea travel in any case. In the easier circumstances of his retirement he could no doubt have afforded it, but he doesn't seem to have been in the least interest in the possibility of it as far as one can see.

The point I am trying to make is that interpreting the significance that the lore, legend, and presence of the sea assumes in Tolkien's world, it is the seashore, the sea's margin, that represents reality; the sea itself is a symbol. The actual practice of seafaring, or sailing, and of life aboard ship, are not Tolkien's, or our concern. Even the exploits of the Númenóreans are seen from a distance, and largely in a critical, sometimes highly critical, spirit. The sea stands for everything that divides the real world from the unseen, imagination from reality, the unconscious, dreaming mind from waking experience, myth from history, and above all, this life from the hereafter. I want to consider how this crucially important image of "the sundering sea", arises and develops in the course of Tolkien's life and work, and also to set it somewhat in the context of romanticism, looked at more widely over the previous century.

It is not Tolkien's first writings, however, but his early drawings and paintings that provide a starting point. Wayne Hammond and Christina Scull, have shown how thoroughly his artistic work, as it developed during the course of his life, is bound up with his writings and his developing conceptions of his "sub-created" world. And in the beginning, his early art stands in front of the gateway which leads to that world. Seashore related subjects make an early appearance in the watercolour of two boys on a beach (dated by Hammond and Scull to 1902) (1995, op. cit. pl. 5) and of a ship at anchor, evidently produced somewhat later (Hammond & Scull, 1992, op. cit. pl. 6). More subjects, from Lyme Regis or Whitby (Hammond & Scull, 1995, op. cit. pls. 8 & 9) occupy him later on in his teens. There is nothing at all surprising about any of this while he is on holiday. But a highly significant stylistic change makes itself felt when, at the age of twenty-two, he tackles the Cornish coast instead. At this time, his artistic output is beginning to comprise, besides topographical or realistic subjects, semi-abstract or imaginary scenes or "visions" which he describes as "ishnesses". It is instructive to observe how the fantastic, sea-sculpted, rock-scapes that provide the subject-matter of two of his topographical works of this period merge into and prepare one for some of the "visionary" works of the same period notably a "seashore" type of vision like "Water, Wind and Sand" (Hammond & Scull, 1995, op. cit. pl. 42). This latter work is associated with the early poem "Sea Chant of an Elder Day", written according to Carpenter (1977, p. 74) on December 4th, 1914, and based on memories of the Cornish holiday of a few months earlier. The poem included the following lines:

> I sat on the ruined margin of the deep-voiced echoing sea
> Whose roaring foaming music crashed in endless cadency
> On the land besieged for ever in an æon of assaults
> And torn in towers and pinnacles and caverned in great vaults.

These lines are interesting in that they introduce the motive of the sea as on impersonal force, alien and disruptive, and in doing so they provide a link with Tolkien's childhood dream image of "the great wave towering up and advancing ineluctably over the trees and green fields, poised to engulf him and all around him". This latter image will make its importance felt later on when the layer of the mythology first introducing Númenor comes to be laid down. At this stage in Tolkien's development, the imagery of the poem and the paintings just mentioned, is linked closely with *The Book of Lost Tales*, especially with the similar imagery which surrounds the "Shoreland Pipers", the Solosimpi, the early counterpart of the Telerin Elves of the more developed mythology. The Solosimpi take up residence in Tol Eressëa, once that "floating island" has been anchored to the sea-bottom by Ossë (in defiance of Ulmo his nominal superior).

In *The Book of Lost Tales*, considered as a whole (except the final Tale, which I will come to in a moment), the sea does not carry any particular significance, beyond contributing to the whole scheme of mythological imagery; it does not, in effect, provide anything more than a picturesque part of the scenery. All three branches of the Elvish peoples, including the Solosimpi, are transported by "floating islands", the others to Valinor itself, by Ulmo, or in opposition by Ossë, as above. The sea only represents a subordinate part of the mythic scheme at this stage, and to begin with the realism that would be aroused by references to actual ship-building or sea voyaging is quite absent. Nevertheless, when the Solosimpi are settled in Tol Eressëa they are instructed by Ulmo in the arts of shipbuilding and navigation, and they become distinguished by their skill in and mastery of them, especially when they also are transported to Valinor.

All the same, they don't appear to do very much in terms of seafaring or substantial voyaging; nor do their successors the Teleri: at any rate if they do, we don't get to hear anything about it. Their delight in sailing perhaps merely expressed itself in what might a little frivolously be interpreted as a series of glorified pub-crawls around the coasts of Aman and the Lonely Isle!

It is with the last of the Lost Tales, which deals with the efforts of Eriol to reach the Lonely Isle, now in his character of Ælfwine of England whom we encountered at the very beginning, at "The Cottage of Lost Play", that the sea, and with it the seashore, begins to take on a significance transcending that of mere stage scenery. He now appears in a new tale as a voyager from a far-distant land, Belerion (Britain), battered and frustrated by the perils and setbacks of the journey. Belerion is overrun by the Forodwaith (the men from the north), who may be equated with the Vikings of historical records; Ælfwine takes ship from the far south-west – in other words Cornwall. Even though all this is overlaid with layer upon layer of legend, there is underlying reality in the idea of Ælfwine as a migrant from our own world, as his Anglo-Saxon name makes clear. Therefore, a structured contrast has been set up between "our world", corresponding to Tolkien's in its guise as "feigned history", and the mythology proper. It is hardly possible to overstate the importance of this stage in the evolution of the "legendarium", as a whole; that is actually an imprecise term because so much of it will eventually be presented in the guise of "feigned history", the convention accepted by readers that the material simply represents a distillation of actual "historical records", which by accident have been handed down to a later Age of the World. It is not too much to say that the confusion of "myth" with "history" is the driving force throughout Tolkien's "sub-" creative life, and that the sea represents the boundary line dividing them.

In the last of the Lost Tales, therefore, the hostility of the "cruel sea" has finally been awakened. Ælfwine only reaches Tol Eressëa after protracted voyaging and repeated false landfalls. The sea separating Belerion from Tol Eressëa and Valinor has become, very nearly, an impassable barrier. The pursuing Forodwaith, who have taken over Belerion, likewise experience shipwrecks and extreme perils. It is nevertheless a notable feature of the Tale that it contains the barest minimum of reference to the actual practice of sailing, its labours, dangers, and frequent disasters. There are descriptions of arrival or departure, but none of actual days at sea. This will remain characteristic of Tolkien's writing throughout the remainder of his life; there is no single major scene in any of his writings actually set on board ship. The practice of seafaring is the mainstay of Aldarion's existence in the (unfinished) tale of the failed relationship with Erendis that provided a turning point in the history of Númenor. Yet while we are told about his long absences at sea, and his departures from and returns to Númenor, we hear nothing about his life as a sailor and sea-captain, or the lives of his crews. To the connoisseur of the genre of "sea-stories", that would have been the most interesting thing about him.

The next major section of Tolkien's creative life represents the periods covered by volumes III and IV of Christopher Tolkien's *The History of Middle-earth*: *The Lays of Beleriand* and *The Shaping of Middle-earth*. These display, conspicuously, a progressive weighting of the material in favour of the history of the Elves of Beleriand and, indeed, concentrate on an extremely limited span of time at the end of which nearly the whole of Beleriand has been overrun by Morgoth. This is reflected in the respective chronologies of Valinor and Beleriand; the former being given in multiple of years. Such events as the departure of the Elves from Valinor, their long march northwards, and their arrival and establishment on the far north-west of Middle-earth, though superficially appearing to occupy a relatively brief space of time, must correspond in mythic terms, to a *Volkwänderung* extending over perhaps several hundred years. Tolkien is being imperceptibly pulled away from his original understanding of his world, purely and simply as mythology, towards something more complex and ambiguous.

Nevertheless, because so much of the *Quenta Silmarillion*, is concerned with events and peoples within Beleriand itself, away from the sea, there is little opportunity for the sea, or the sea-longing, to develop as a motive in its own right, and likewise the lays of Beleriand themselves do not provide anything in the way of subject-matter or scope. There are, however, two important instances where the sea does play, whether expressly or by implication, a major role: the episode of the Kinslaying and the subsequent theft of the ships of the Teleri; and that of the crossing of the Helcaraxë and that of the subsequent burning of the ships by order of Fëanor. These episodes are associated with the curse of the Noldorin exiles proclaimed in "The Prophecy of the North", which will resonate throughout the First Age. The Helcaraxë once crossed, the Noldor, unrepentant, are (until the eventual mission of Eärendil to the Valar) excluded from returning to Aman. The sea that separates Aman from Middle-earth, from having been initially an impassable barrier, or virtually so, is in the process of becoming an impermissible one.

The next stage in the sequence consists of the early account of the Fall of Númenor contained in volume V of *The History of Middle-earth* series, *The Lost Road* (Tolkien, 1987). If one looks retrospectively at Tolkien's writing from beginning to end, this appears as a watershed in his creative life as much as *The Hobbit* does, written as it was at very much the same time as the latter was published. Christopher Tolkien has shown (Tolkien, 1997, pp. 7-10) that the inception of the "Númenórean" complex of tales arises directly from the agreement Tolkien made with C.S. Lewis that they would each write, respectively, a story about "time travel" and "space travel". The essentials of the story of Númenor and its fall of course are familiar. Those among Men who have aided the Elves and the Valar in the war against Morgoth are rewarded with "The Land of Gift", the island Númenor, in the seas west of Middle-earth. They are forbidden to sail to the west, initially beyond Tol Eressëa, but finally, out of sight of their west coasts; after many generations they rebel against the ban, at the instigation of Sauron; in consequence Númenor is overwhelmed, and Tol Eressëa and Valinor are removed from the circles of the world; sailors to the west can now only reach fresh lands and eventually return to their starting point; the world is "made round", and the former "straight road" to the Uttermost West only remains in legend, permitted only to those Elves who are leaving Middle-earth for ever. The sea, therefore, has become a total and impassable barrier between the seen and unseen worlds.

The successive texts embodying the legend, as we now have them laid out for us in *The History of Middle-earth*, reveal the remarkable series of changes and variants which Tolkien introduced into the outline of the story as it evolved, especially at a time, seemingly early in 1946, when *The Lord of the Rings* still lay unfinished, and "The Notion Club Papers" had been conceived. In the end, later on in his life, with the *Akallabêth*, Tolkien largely returns to the original conception of *The Fall of Númenor* but also incorporates the new and additional material that entered the story with the *Drowning of Andúnië* texts of the period of "The Notion Club Papers". Christopher Tolkien interprets all these inconsistencies and contradictions between these successive rewritings of the basic story as indicating that Tolkien had come to regard them as co-existing in that they could represent varying traditions surviving in the Third Age, especially traditions among Men of varying groups and origins.

(Tolkien, 1992, pp. 505-7) A letter quoted by Christopher Tolkien here, (Carpenter, 1981, No. 151, p. 186) illustrates this position further.

> "Middle-earth ... lay then just as it does. In fact, just as it does, round and inescapable. The new situation, established at the beginning of the Third Age, leads on eventually and inevitably to ordinary History, and we here see the process culminating. If you or I or any of the mortal men (or Hobbits) of Frodo's day had set out over sea, west, we should, as now, eventually have come back (as now) to our starting point. Gone was the 'mythological' time when Valinor ... existed physically in the Uttermost West, or the Eldaic (Elvish) immortal Isle of Eressëa; or the Great Isle of Westernesse (Númenor – Atlantis) ... etc."

The especial significance of the passage, and the ultimate form of the Akallabêth, is that they complete the transition from mythology to history; "feigned history", of course, but, as the passage indicates, Tolkien thought of his "History" as leading straight on towards "real" history. We have, in the course of journeying through *The History of Middle-earth*, turned our stance through one-hundred-and-eighty degrees; instead of regarding mythology as a prelude from which history will ultimately evolve, we are now, as it were from the other end, looking backwards through ages of history towards the distant prospect of myth. And the essential symbol of this is the sea, not the everyday sea which encircles the "world made round" and which has no special significance, but the former sea, now "the sundering sea", which marks the boundary that separates us from myth, the attainable from the unattainable.

The time of writing of *The Notion Club Papers*, is very

much that of transition between the two extremes, and it has several interesting accompaniments:

- Arundel Lowdhams description of his father Edwin Lowdham's sailing away into the Atlantic in 1947 in his boat, the "Earendel", and never returning. He had previously sailed extensively about the coasts of Ireland and north-west Europe, and had always been subject to restlessness and "the sea-longing".
- The great storm described as occurring in 1987, and the narrative of Lowdham and Jeremy, after their disappearance and return, of their travel around the west of Ireland and Scotland and ultimately, back to Porlock in Somerset; incidentally, they appear to have travelled on land for much of the time. The remarkable feature of their story is their description of the great waves, "high as hills", which rolled over the Aran Islands and well inland from Ireland's west coasts, and yet were like phantoms and did no material damage. We are faced with somewhat of an inconsistency here, because while the sea at this point is clearly "symbolic" and not of the real worlds, the storm that breaks over Oxford in the midst of which Lowdham and Jeremy disappear, although in one sense a symbolic counterpart of the cataclysm that overwhelms Númenor, is a real storm that does quite a lot of physical damage.
- The poem "Imram", and its predecessor, recounting the voyage of St. Brendan from the west of Ireland to the far west and the visions he experiences. However, it is the latter, and not the voyage itself, which is the focus of interest, and the saint does not vanish out of sight

and mind, but does return ultimately to Ireland, if only to die there.

The mature expression of the concept of the "sundering sea", finds itself most poignantly in the concluding scene of *The Lord of the Rings*, with the image of the waves lapping on the shores of Middle-earth, in counterpoint with that of Frodo's departure for an inaccessible destination, along the unseen "Straight Road". Of course the body of narrative in *The Lord of the Rings*, has not provided much opportunity for enlarging the imagery of the "sundering sea", beyond the occasional reference to the departure of the Elves, "sailing, sailing" into the west leaving Middle-earth for ever; or the dream visions of Frodo himself; conversely the very idea of the sea, real or symbolic, is anathema to ordinary hobbits, who turned their faces from the hills in the west. But this final scene with the poem subtitled "Frodo's Dreme" and "The Sea-Bell", completes the progress that had started out with Tolkien's water colours and drawings of his schooldays.

"The Sea-Bell" is the late, mature version of a poem originally entitled "Looney" that had appeared many years before,[1] it recounts the story of a wonderer who is drawn to voyage west over sea to a distant land of "Faërie", his inability to meet with or communicate with its inhabitants and his eventual return to his own world, where he finds himself still under an impalpable curse, unable to converse or communicate with those around him. The implication is that he has broken some indefinable ban (as the Númenóreans broke the ban of the Valar), in journeying to what seems to be, in retrospect a

1. In 1934. (Flieger, 1997, pp. 208 et seq.)

forbidden land; where its former beauty and inviting aspect turn on a sudden wintry desolation. However, these overtones of loneliness, and guilt at succumbing to the "sea-longing", and journeying to the "forbidden land", only enter with the mature version of the poem, which accordingly, like the final scene of *The Lord of the Rings*, displays the development of Tolkien's thought over a long period.

The entire concept of "the sundering sea", a symbolic divide between this world and the hereafter, or, if you like, between reality and the imagination, is a profoundly Romantic one, and it may be of some interest to end by seeking some kind of a parallel within the context of nineteenth century Romanticism in general. Certainly it is very much in tune with the Romantic tendency to identify Nature in all its aspects, and the phenomena of Nature, with the emotions and aspirations of mankind, and in a religious sense, with man's relationship with the divine. Likewise, for instance, German romantic poetry is from time to time apt to celebrate the poet's longing for some "blessed realm", beyond the confines of the everyday world. It is though, not very easy to find a close counterpart of parallel for Tolkien's concept of the sea as a purely symbolic barrier. The realities of seafaring, and the attendant dangers, tended to intrude themselves too insistently. J.M.W. Turner painted the sea in its most hostile and disruptive aspects again and again, but he was brought up in London's dockland; his ships are real ships, and he knew what sailing was all about. It is, though, with the work of a contemporary of Turner, another artist, in a way his counterpart, that a kind of precedent can perhaps be found.

The painter in question is Caspar David Friedrich (1774-

1840)[2], of whom Tolkien almost quite certainly never heard; he was almost unknown in this country until the early 1970s. He was born and brought up in Pomerania, on the Baltic coast, although he spent much of his life in Dresden, where he came into contact with many of the literary circles of the time. His drawings and paintings of the sea-shore, and of ships and shipping do start out realistically and straightforwardly (as of course in their way do Tolkien's, in the art of his schooldays and up to his "Cornish" period). He was deeply and profoundly religious and prone to read Christian symbolism into almost every feature or manifestation of Nature that he painted, the moon, rainbows, the seasons, and so forth. The seashore provided a considerable proportion of his subject matter; a famous instance is "A Monk by the Seashore", a strange and visionary conception in which a solitary figure placed on a wide strand stares out at a huge expanse of sea, seemingly into infinity. Others show figures in the dress of the period (or old German costume), including the painter himself, sitting or standing on the seashore gazing on over the sea at spectral ships which advance towards the picture plane or recede from it, and which are thought to symbolise "the stages of life"[3] (the title of one such painting) (Börsch-Supan 1974, op. cit. illus. pl. 52) or man's relationship with death and the hereafter.

---

2. As to Friedrich see Helmut Börsch-Supan *Caspar David Friedrich* (English edition. Thames & Hudson 1974 – originally published in German; Prestel-Verlag, Munich).
3. See also "Moonrise over the sea" (Börsch-Supan 1974, op. cit. illus. pl. 34).

Bibliography

Carpenter, Humphrey, 1977, *J.R.R. Tolkien: A Biography*, George Allen & Unwin, London.
---, 1981, *The Letters of J.R.R. Tolkien*, George Allen & Unwin, London.

Flieger, Verlyn, 1997, *A Question of Time: Tolkien's Road to Faërie,* Kent State University Press, Ohio.

Hammond, Wayne & Christina Scull, 1995, *Tolkien: Artist & Illustrator*, HarperCollins Publishers, London.

Tolkien, John & Priscilla, 1992, *The Tolkien Family Album*, The Houghton Mifflin Co. Boston.

Tolkien, J.R.R., 1987, *The Lost Road and other writings*, Unwin Hyman Ltd., London.
---, 1992, *Sauron Defeated*, HarperCollins Publishers, London.